PRAISE FOR *BLOOMI*

"Beautifully written, filled with family conflict, love and suspense, the story of Jacomena Maybeck is the tale of every woman and her struggles to find her voice and create a life on her own terms."

—LOUISE NAYER, author of *Burned: A Memoir*, an Oprah Great Read

"Navigating widowhood and grappling with the onset of old age, Maybeck embraces her independence and freely explores all artistic inquiries. . . . A reverential celebration of a feisty woman with a zest for growth, art, community, and dynamic living. This careful consideration of an extraordinary life emphasizes creative expression and the strength of womanhood."

—BOOKLIFE REVIEWS

"Many books deal with Berkeley's architectural roots and Maybeck's influence. *Blooming in Winter* successfully intertwines Berkeley's architecture and social history, seamlessly integrating architectural design with family combat and a woman's fight for and right to independence."

—LESLIE M. FREUDENHEIM, author of *Building with Nature: Inspiration for the Arts and Crafts Home*

"Planted in the soil of the Maybeck family, *Blooming in Winter* is an absorbing tale and a graceful retelling of a woman's life. Widowed at age sixty-one, Jacomena Maybeck seeks—and finds—her own identity as an artist and storyteller."

—SANDRA BUTLER, co-author of *It Never Ends: Mothering Middle-Aged Daughters*

"[This] biography focuses on a venerable woman who left her mark on Berkeley, California. Valois' careful selection of quotes from Maybeck's contradictory, 'Rashomon-like' diaries are deployed to great effect, furthering the vision of a charming woman anyone would love to know. . . . [T]he account feels like a nostalgic conversation about a deeply loved, mutual friend. An engaging portrait. . . ."

—*KIRKUS REVIEWS*

"In *Blooming in Winter*, . . . Valois introduces us to her friend and muse, Jacomena Maybeck, and reveals an insider's vision of Maybeck life and architecture. Carefully curated and based on letters, diaries, interviews, and extensive research, Valois's collage is a compelling portrait of a fascinating woman who provides a glimpse into how to balance dark thoughts with small pleasures and live fully at any age."

—RUTH O. SAXTON, author of *The Book of Old Ladies,* and Professor Emerita of English at Mills College

"While *Blooming in Winter* presents the story of Jacomena's life in a legendary family, it shares themes that are universal to all women—the challenges of fitting in while maintaining independence in a circle of large personalities, the struggle to find creative outlets and realizing your passion, and gracefully aging while change is all around you."

—JAN BERCKEFELDT, Executive Director, Maybeck Foundation

"*Blooming in Winter* portrays my mother, Jacomena Maybeck, as she was in life. With a fine ear for my mother's wit, a wink at her quirkiness, and a knowledge of her secrets, Pam Valois reveals the secrets of a good old age."

—ADRIANA (CHERRY) MAYBECK NITTLER

BLOOMING IN WINTER

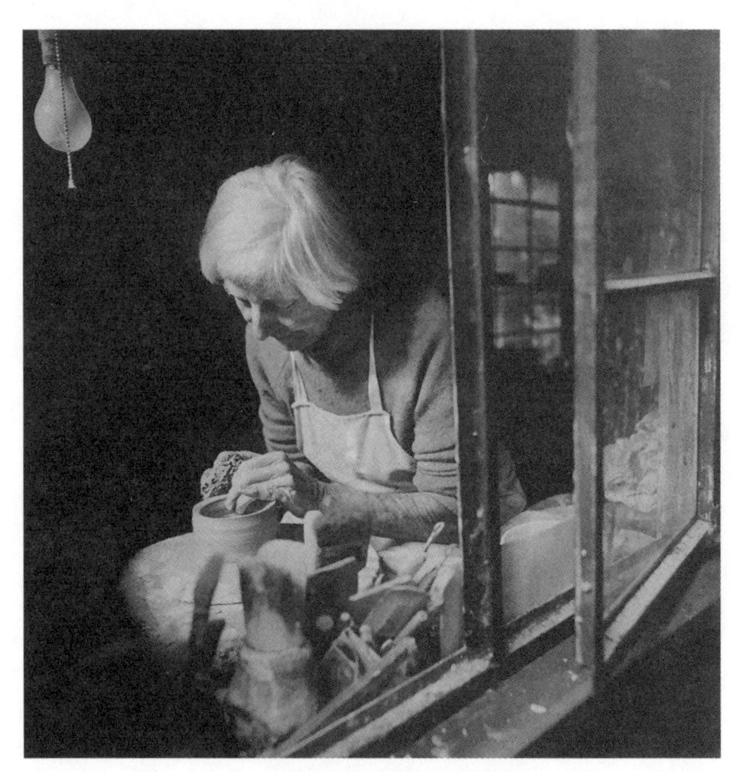

Jacomena Maybeck, 1978.

Photograph by Pam Valois.

BLOOMING IN WINTER

THE STORY OF A REMARKABLE TWENTIETH-CENTURY WOMAN

PAMELA VALOIS

SHE WRITES PRESS

Published 2021
Printed in the United States of America
Print ISBN: 978-1-64742-116-8
E-ISBN: 978-1-64742-117-5
Library of Congress Control Number: 2020925551

For information, address:
She Writes Press
1569 Solano Ave #546
Berkeley, CA 94707

Interior design by Tabitha Lahr

She Writes Press is a division of SparkPoint Studio, LLC.

Names and identifying characteristics have been changed to protect the privacy of certain individuals.

For Lloyd, with whom I shared
the joy of knowing Jacomena.

I think that to one in sympathy with nature,
each season, in its turn, seems the loveliest.

—Mark Twain

CONTENTS

PROLOGUE

I wake to screeching Steller's jays competing for a soak in the water bowl. Climbing the worn wooden stairs in search of coffee, I'm greeted by the light glowing on the etched beams, and the tall windows filling the living room with sunshine and hope. Sometimes I see her—Jacomena van Huizen Maybeck—sitting at the head of what is now my dining room table, planning her day on a yellow pad of paper, or writing to the twins. The spinning spiders of her day have left the rafters. Outside the south window, robins queue for a bath, hiding in the last of the sycamore leaves while they wait. Pepe whistles to be uncovered, looking forward to sharing breakfast. Lloyd has made coffee!

In March 2013, I moved to 2751 Buena Vista Way, the Wallen and Jacomena Maybeck House,[1] with my husband, Lloyd Linford, and our parrot, Pepe. The house is still often called "Jackie's house" because so many people in Berkeley and in the wider arts and architecture community in the East Bay knew and revered her. Jackie, as she liked to be called, has been a uniquely important person in my life for more than forty years, including the years since her death in 1996.

This morning, sitting at the dining room table admiring my neighbor's flowering magnolia framed by the great north window, I find myself wishing once again that I had asked her more about her life. I knew her only in her late years, and am left with so many questions. Where did she come from, and what had shaped this venerable woman we loved?

In 1977, I learned from a friend that Jacomena Maybeck was renting out the Maybeck Cottage across the street from her home at 2751. As Lloyd and I opened the Cottage gate for our first visit, a woman in her midseventies, dressed in a halter top and shorts, came into view. She was up on the roof with a tar pot and a trowel. Our future landlady had a long face, twinkling blue eyes, and a shock of brilliant white hair, cut short. We had never met anyone quite like her. She seemed to like us, but wanted to visit our San Francisco flat to get more of a sense of whether we would "fit." She came for lunch—I'd made a quiche—and was immediately romanced by our young parrot, Pepe, who jumped on her hand and gently pecked at her Navajo turquoise rings. Lloyd and I exchanged incredulous looks: Pepe never liked anyone right off the bat. Jackie rented us the Cottage, and we felt we'd died and gone to heaven. Our threadbare Persian rugs and overstuffed secondhand furniture fit right in. We had a winter living room for cold nights and a breezy summer living room for warm ones. The Cottage is settled in an oasis of greenery with a view straight across the Bay to the Golden Gate Bridge.

Those years in the Cottage were idyllic. Pepe perched in the apple tree until the day that Fat Cat Rudy scared him and he flew into a thorn bush, hurting his eye. Lloyd, a postdoctoral fellow at Kaiser Permanente, would flop on the couch with a manuscript on his lap. After our work-days, we'd sit in the garden or the cozy coffee nook, and on

The Cottage, 1977.

Photograph by Pam Valois.

weekends, visit Jackie in her sunny house uphill across the street. Supper at Jackie's might be a potato and salad. She would heat up the great room by burning brush that she'd gathered from the neighborhood.

By 1977, Jackie had been a widow for fifteen years, and her approach to life inspired me. She knew how to throw a pot, garden in company of deer and skunks, wield an ax or a sickle, and make plum jam. She took relationships seriously and had many longstanding friends. She'd become the expert on her father-in-law, architect Bernard Maybeck, hosting house tours and being interviewed for books and articles. Alan Temko, an architectural critic of the period, wrote that Jackie, whom he called Maybeck's "true spiritual daughter," helped shape the "intangible Maybeck quality. . . as much as any of them except [Maybeck's wife] Annie."[2]

Jackie kept a daily log in her large, bold handwriting. She read an excerpt to me: "Billowy clouds today; pink flowers starting to bloom—I hope my 1980 is bright. I woke up to a blue sky and a chance for outdoor work, taming the overgrown bushes and moving in my new student—there he is, with a big red beard and a guitar."[3] She called her morning routine her worry time: "If you wake up and write in your book, 'it's horrible weather' then you can just go on from there—it helps." Jackie knew how to balance dark thoughts with small pleasures: "My floors are dirty; Russia is piling soldiers into Afghanistan, but there is one pure green and yellow primrose in bloom."

We loved receiving notes slipped under our door: "Happy Christmas to the prettiest and the handsomest neighbor—guess who? I'm over my good [pottery] Sale and my usual laryngitis after it—forgive me if I just nod and smile for a while. Love, Jackie."

Jackie's Christmas cards included line drawings and prose printed on colored paper. She wrote whimsical stories based on her own cats, such as "Cattail: Emily & Peter," in which the cats gossip about neighbors. Her descriptions were magical: "Berkeley is green. Irish green, yellow green, bronze green, and plain green. A sea of leaves, a moving ocean of twigs and branches full of leaves."[4] When Jackie

Jacomena's Christmas card, n.d.

Drawing courtesy of Maybeck family.

Jacomena's Christmas card, n.d.

Drawing courtesy of Maybeck family.

traveled, she'd send home watercolored postcards of gardens and houses.

Jackie introduced us to her friends and neighbors at long, charming dinner parties. Her front door was never locked; "Come on upstairs," she'd say to guests. Neighbors used the back door, climbing a dirt path. We drank wine at her broad wooden table while the sun set across the Bay. We sat on benches and she sat at the head of the table in her tall ladder chair with arms. The kitchen, dining room, and living room were all in one grand room designed by Bernard Maybeck, who said, "I don't want my wife out in the kitchen slaving away while I'm with the company. I want her part of the company."[5]

I was in my midthirties and knew just a few people, outside of family, over seventy. Because I was barely aware of the stereotypes in my head, Jackie's vitality continually surprised me. A different view of aging and what was possible began to coalesce. I was studying photography, and tried to capture her essence as she spun her potting wheel, worked in her garden, or stoked a fire in her huge fireplace. She introduced me to her friends—Flo Jury, Ruth Pennell, and Kay Seidel, among others—and I photographed them as well. These women seemed to love being retired, not just from jobs but from burdensome family roles as well. The topic of aging seldom came up among them. My conversations about these experiences with friends my own age suggested how much our assumptions about aging informed our relationships, and even the possibility of relationships with older adults, and how much a dread of getting old existed in the back of our heads. Jackie's friends introduced me to their own version of Jackie, an older woman who inspired them and shattered their stereotypes too.

Jacomena at 2751 Buena Vista Way, 1979.
Photograph by Pam Valois.

An exciting project began to take shape. Through a partnership with the writer Charlotte Painter, it would become our book, *Gifts of Age: Portraits and Essays of 32 Remarkable Women.*[6] Jackie, and a wish to be just like her when I got old, inspired the book.

Now, years later, I'm close to the age Jackie was when I met her. I recently reread her *People & Places: A Memoir*, published in 1992 when she was ninety-one years old. The last chapter begins:

> *Here I am free of a job. Retired. Well, now what? What is there in myself to work with, to enjoy with? Really, age is a damn nuisance. You have to work harder for everything. But magic things still happen!*[7]

Jacomena in her garden, 1980.

Photograph by Pam Valois.

In my own life, part of the answer to Jackie's big question—*Now what?*—was answered by good luck. My husband and I found ourselves in a position to buy this wonderful house that was hers for so many years. It's a house that celebrates life in all its seasons, just as Jackie did. Her dedication to family and friends, her creativity, optimism, and talent for enjoying a simple life made so much difference to me through my child-rearing days. Now in my seventies, I see the gifts she gave me in a different light. In this remembrance of her, I want to share a more complete and nuanced story of her life, one that suggests what she has meant to me and others who loved her. She's gone from the scene, but her house, with all its magic, has a life and history of its own. That, too, is a part of this story.

In my exploration of Jackie and her history, her books, *Maybeck: The Family View*[8] and *The 4-Year Stretch*[9] (written with Florence Jury), have been invaluable sources along with the memoir mentioned earlier. Jackie's diaries and letters reveal more about what was on her mind, as she is frank and reflective in writing them. Although I was thrilled to read her diaries, I am surprised that she never destroyed them. In *Revelations*,[10] Mary Jane Moffat and Charlotte Painter culled the diaries of hundreds of twentieth-century women, defining the diary as a valid literary form—one that for most women was the only available outlet for honest expression. For Jackie, her recorded private passions and insights were a guide through many difficult times.

In 1980, I interviewed Jackie in her home, while working on *Gifts of Age*. Quotations from the interview appear often in this portrait of her, so that the reader may experience her unique voice. All quotes not attributed to other sources are from this interview. Various people's accounts, and even Jackie's own stories about her life, were sometimes inconsistent. Like the wonderful Akira Kurosawa film, *Rashomon*, there's clearly more than one way to tell this story. My conversations with Jackie's daughters, Cherry and Sheila, her grandchildren, and neighbors who knew her helped me develop a richer and fuller portrait of her.

SPRING

A MAGIC PLACE

Where did Jacomena Adriana van Huizen come from, and how did she become Jackie Maybeck? In her 1992 memoir, she writes, "In this family [this question is] mostly asked of a Maybeck, as though I had been found in a cabbage! But I love to look back to my parents and let the beautiful Dutch names flow over my tongue. My father, Piet Jan Rensius van Huizen. My mother, Helene Kleyn-Schoorel—she was always called Lane."[1]

Jackie was born in Surabaya, Java, where Piet (called Pieter in this story) worked as a sugar chemist. They lived in a concrete house with one side completely open. Helene, who took up the sarong and a white linen jacket, had a great sense of adventure which Java called out in her. Jackie wrote, "I arrived somehow on March 19, 1901—though Mother's doctor got drunk and couldn't be found!"[2] Jacomena was named for her two grandmothers, Jacomena and Adriana.

The family moved back to Holland when Jackie was seven months old, and her brother, Piet, was born when she was two years old. Jackie describes her brother as "the pretty one with curly hair and bright blue eyes. I felt he always got the best of everything—if we each had a vegetable garden, his vegetables grew tallest. In the Dutch tradition, he was the very important boy, and girls weren't anything."

Helene and Pieter van Huizen, 1900.

Photograph courtesy of Maybeck family.

Helene van Huizen in Surabaya, Java, 1901.

Photograph courtesy of Maybeck family.

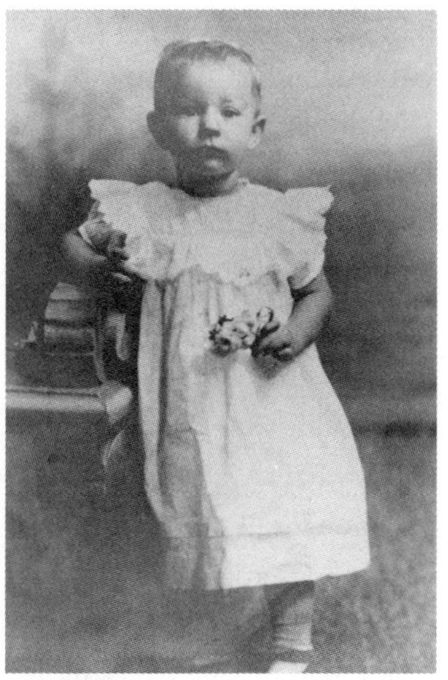

Jacomena in Holland, 1902.

Photograph courtesy of Maybeck family.

Left to right: Adriana Kleyn-Schoorel and Tante Maal, Holland, n.d.

Photograph courtesy of Maybeck family.

In those years of early childhood, Jackie's family lived in Holland with grandmother "Oma" Kleyn-Schoorel while her father traveled for work. She frequently saw her father's mother, who, at age eighty-four, still bicycled to visit friends. Jackie enjoyed the gatherings with her large extended family. She remembers sitting on the floor surrounded by wonderful little boxes, pencils and pads, and strings and clips. Perhaps this was the beginning of her love of drawing.

Jackie's maternal uncle, Nick Kleyn-Schoorel, who was far away in California searching for gold, convinced young Jackie's family to join him. In 1907, the van Huizens sailed from Rotterdam to the snowy port of New York, then traveled by train to Los Angeles where Jackie's mother wrote back to her sisters, "This is the most beautiful place I've ever seen!"[3] Barely six years old, and speaking little English, Jackie stayed close to her mom. "My mother was always my very good companion . . . I look like her, I think, except she had curly hair, which I always envied."[4]

By the time Jackie's family arrived in Southern California, the "gold mine" had petered out. Uncle Nick was broke, and Pieter decided to put his money into finishing a house in Northern California, where the family lived for a while, then sold it to raise cash. Eventually, Pieter found work as a chemist in Crockett, northeast of San Francisco, entailing yet another move. Jackie says in her memoir, "I went to school there, to the fifth grade . . . is that possible? There must have been something in between. Another house, probably. More money gone."[5] These four years of not knowing where they would settle challenged the little family. They had abandoned a comfortable life in Holland for the promise of gold, and Helene had decided to follow her wandering husband to the new world. The photo on page 8, taken in 1910, shows a confident and undaunted big sister. Perhaps Jackie had made new friends, learned English, and was getting used to expecting the unexpected.

Piet and Jacomena, 1905.

Photograph courtesy of Maybeck family.

Piet and Jacomena, 1910.

Photograph courtesy of Maybeck family.

Piet and Jacomena, n.d.

Photograph courtesy of Maybeck family.

Then Uncle Nick changed the picture again. He had married the daughter of a Berkeley professor, Isaak Flagg, who owned a country house in the hills west of the Northern California town of Ukiah. The house was built in 1909 by Bernard Maybeck. Already widely known as "California's most eccentric, visionary, and romantic architect,"[6] he went on to build over 150 buildings, the majority of them being distinctive houses in Berkeley. Maybeck would soon become a luminary of American architecture, best known for his San Francisco masterpiece, the Palace of Fine Arts, built in 1915.

Nick and his wife, Amy, frequently stayed in the Flagg home, where Jackie's family often visited them, camping near the house and exploring the countryside. At around the same time, Bernard and Annie Maybeck themselves were looking for a country property. Jackie describes her first encounter with them:

> *One day in 1911, the Klein-Schoorels and the Van Huizens were cooking and cleaning up a storm—the Maybecks were coming up and they might buy land! . . . The Maybecks came down the trail shouting and singing. . . . Maybeck's Pooh Bear figure, the beard, the sparkling eyes were all there and stayed in my life from then on.*[7]

The Maybecks ended up buying two thousand acres on Pine Ridge Road, some ten miles west of Ukiah, and eventually built a small log cabin there. The kids worked on it together, rolling stones for a fireplace, eating fried oatmeal, and drinking the fresh, sweet spring water. Jackie's relationship with the Maybecks would last a lifetime. She recounted her first impression of Bernard. "He was very kind; he was sociable. He was interested in people; he was gentle."[8] The Maybecks' handsome son, Wallen, was thirteen, and Jackie, age ten, became good friends with him and his adventuresome nine-year-old sister, Kerna. Jackie had her eye on Wallen:

> *I couldn't play with Wallen. But I could look at him, and admire him. And I did. For many years we all rode and hiked and sang together in the sunsets. I sat beside Wallen in a shy glow of love and admiration, and deep inside I knew I would some day marry him.*[9]

Wallen Maybeck, 1910.

Photograph courtesy of Maybeck family.

Wallen Maybeck, 1915.

Photograph courtesy of Maybeck family.

Jackie's parents, too, fell in love with the country around Ukiah, and in 1913 they bought one hundred acres of land from Uncle Nick on Pine Ridge Road, near the Maybecks' land. Jackie recalled, "Dad acquired his part [of the land], sort of by accident, whenever Uncle Nick needed money."[10]

Piet, Pieter, and Jacomena, near Ukiah, California, 1910.

Photograph courtesy of Maybeck family.

Jacomena, Helene, and Piet, near Ukiah, California, 1910.

Photograph courtesy of Maybeck family.

Initially, the van Huizens rented a house in Ukiah while Jackie's father went off to Cuba to earn money working as a sugar chemist. He was frequently away for work, and Jackie's bond with him was not strong. "My father was quite dashing. . . . I thought he was a nice person to have around and that was about it."[11] When World War I broke out in 1914, Pieter nearly didn't get back, as he wasn't yet a citizen. Finally, in 1916, the family broke ground on their land, calling it the "ranch."

For Jackie, now fifteen years old, this project was the beginning of a deep-rooted love for designing and building houses, something she would do many times in the future.

> *Now we had to make a dirt road to our hundred acres and build a house. . . . First a level path to a large flat knoll, not too far from a never-dry spring. No one could live up in that country without a good spring for water. . . . We decided on a homesite, on the north edge of the flat, leaving the south and east ends for mother's garden.*
>
> *Next we made a path up the hill to a little forest of pines. . . . Pieter and I trimmed and peeled them and all four of us carried them down the hill. Too steep for the horse. Enough poles to make the framework for the house.*[12]

The ranch would become the secure base Jackie had lacked since leaving Holland, a shelter for her Dutch family as they gradually accommodated to America. She would return to this base again and again over the next several decades.

The house began to come together, and somehow they got Helene's piano inside. Jackie and her brother each had a horse, so she and her mother made divided riding skirts for themselves because few women wore pants in those days. Although the van Huizens called their home a ranch, it was not a typical working ranch with livestock and crops. Helene grew vegetables and flowers on her half acre of garden under the oak trees. A large orchard eventually yielded bushels of fruit, for which passing hunters traded venison, and neighbors traded eggs. Jackie remembered a winter when the road was washed out and they survived on canned peaches and a large sack of dried beans.[13]

While Helene worked to make the rustic house comfortable, serving afternoon tea from her silver tea set, young Jackie would drive the horse and buggy into town for weekly supplies as the boys on horseback "romped along shooting at road signs all the way. In town [Ukiah] the sheriff made them put those guns away."[14]

Hoping to build a community, Uncle Nick had returned to Holland to convince friends from his boyhood to join him in California. Jackie's parents must have been excited to read his announcement in the *Ukiah Republican Press*, promising to return with "people of the very best class, refined and educated." Each ten-acre lot would be frost-free, with a magnificent view, a road, and water, and Nick would build them a bungalow "that will be the envy of your weekend visitors; one of the showplaces of the state."[15] Later newspaper articles referred to a "Dutch colony," that in fact included only the van Huizens, Uncle Nick and his family, and another family named the Hegenvelds.

Although the ranch never yielded a nickel for the family's livelihood, for Jackie "it was simply a magic place":[16]

The Ridge lay to the west and sometimes white fog floated over it. Down in our meadow there were little woods of Manzanita trees. Red trunks, and little bell flowers in January. You knew where they were when you heard bees buzzing. Spring was mad with wildflowers. Summer sizzled with heat and was canning time. . . . Autumn crisped the air, and we cut wood for winter. Winter was weather and isolation. [17]

Jacomena and "White Horse," n.d.

Photograph courtesy of Maybeck family.

The ranch, Pine Ridge Road,
Mendocino County, California.
Drawing by Sheila Bathurst.

Jackie's father usually spent the long summer months away, working in the sugar mills, while Helene, Jackie, and Piet held down the ranch. For an urban dweller like me, it is hard to imagine a woman and two teenagers living in such a remote place. Summers were so hot that the family worked only in the mornings, quitting by noon. "After a long morning of peach peeling, I lay flat on the couch and had my fill of blue sky and glossy green leaves."[18] In the afternoons, Mrs. van Huizen would read aloud while Jackie sewed. They would enjoy the cool garden after dinner and plan the next day's projects. Mrs. van Huizen had always wanted to live in town, but Jackie wrote that she never complained about the isolation on the ranch, "and occasionally, something happened":

> *I heard a queer persistent sound. Suspicious, I peered over the kitchen door and shouted for a flashlight and gun. Mother held the light. Under the bench lay a big rattle-snake, rattling furiously at a tiny curious yellow kitten. He stuck his head out and I shot him. The dog went crazy. We turned the bench over and I cut off his head with a hoe and put the miserable thing in the stove.*[19]

Later that week, her rattlesnake story brought forth not only sympathy from the neighbors, but offerings, too: "I now have six boxes of .22 shells and one of shotgun cartridges."[20]

During the school year, Jackie lived in the Ukiah homes of her mother's various friends, as the ranch was an hour away on a narrow dirt road. The Benson family in particular was important to Jackie. She began "our passionate high school love"[21] with the oldest son, Huntington. In addition to often spending the school week with the Bensons and their seven children, Jackie frequently spent weekends with them:

> *I had to walk ten miles, or somebody had to come with a horse and buggy to get me. . . . [Dr. Benson] would read to us while we had our salads, and then the hot dinner would come. . . . Then the girls would wash the dishes, and the boys went out in the half-dark and milked the cows. Pails of foamy milk came in. When the chores were done, we all came in, put on a record, and danced. Wonderful!*[22]

Jackie credits Dr. Benson, a minister, with awakening her intellectual life and urging her to attend college. While some of the Benson offspring went off to Pomona College in Southern California, Jackie, needing money, sat with fourteen others for a county teacher's credential exam. The newspaper headline the next day stated, "Only Four Pass. The tests were very difficult."[23] As one of the four to earn the credential, Jackie taught at a fourteen-student grammar school on Pine Ridge for two years. "Some of the students were teenage boys. . . . It was like driving a team of very spirited horses. I was just twenty!"[24] She made $130 a month, saving every dime. Then, "I had two choices for college—Pomona and Huntington—Berkeley and Wallen."[25]

Jackie chose Berkeley. "I loved the idea of going to Pomona with Huntington and Geo and Dirk, but I loved Wallen, too. It was a great decision, and there was pain in it."[26] Wallen, who had already graduated from college, worked as an electrical engineer for the telephone company in San Francisco. The Maybecks lived in the Berkeley hills, at 2701 Buena Vista Way, in a big wooden home designed by Bernard Maybeck and built in 1907 after the San Francisco earthquake. Jackie spent a summer with them in 1921, and described the house as "a glamorous place, a sleeping porch for each bedroom, two fireplaces, a raised dining-room, and a kitchen absolutely full of dishes."[27] Robin Pennell, who grew up in this neighborhood with Maybecks of several generations, declared, "The house was so big, you could see it from San Francisco!"[28]

LEARNING A WAY OF LIFE

In September 1923, Jackie—an optimistic country girl and the daughter of intrepid immigrants—took the train south with Mary Benson to begin her college life.

> *The train clopped along tooting through the tunnels and the little towns. . . . Until San Rafael, then suddenly the sharp prick of eucalyptus and a mysterious breath of fog on the skin.*[1]

At the University of California, Berkeley, she met Florence Jury, who would become a lifelong friend. When my husband and I knew them in their late seventies, they depended on each other. Both widows, they called each other every morning to talk about plans for the day or breakfast down the hill on Shattuck Avenue. Flo described meeting Jackie in their freshman year:

> *Sitting directly across the table from me was a tall, slender girl with curly golden hair and blue eyes the shade of the*

> *northern summer sky. Her face was different, not pretty, but arresting and unforgettable in its planes and contours.*
>
> *It was no time at all before we were smoking an after-dinner cigaret [sic] under the outside stairs. . . . There was so much to talk about.*[2]

Jackie added: "We were just freshmen, and all eyes and ears and emotions."[3] Suddenly, she was in a world of girls.

When Jackie came to Berkeley, the university was already considered one of America's premier institutions of higher learning. UC Berkeley was on the map and was the heart of the community, much as it is today. The school had been coeducational since 1870, unusual for American universities at the time. California's (male) voters, however, did not believe that attaining the age of majority was enough to qualify a woman to vote. They defeated a measure to establish female suffrage in 1896. Fifteen years later, just in time for Jackie's generation, California became the sixth state in the United States to enfranchise women, presaging the adoption of the Nineteenth Amendment in 1920.

Having won the right to vote, the modern women of the twenties were exploring and adopting new values. They bobbed their hair, shortened their skirts, drank cocktails, and smoked. They mingled openly with men and burst onto the college scene in larger numbers than ever before. Corsets were swapped in favor of loose-fitting dresses that expressed their carefree spirit. Flo wrote, "There were books that spoke directly to us—explained us, the 'Flaming Youth' [a popular book and movie] generation, to ourselves, and provided our catch phrases, our shibboleths."[4]

Jackie "tingled with excitement" as she stood in long lines to sign up for classes. "The first walk up Telegraph and

Left to right: Kay Morris, Irma Nielsen, Flo Jury, Jacomena, 1925.

Photograph courtesy of Maybeck family.

through Sather Gate was walking into a dream. Boys sat on the walls over the creek and eyed one. The creek gurgled and the blue sky arched to the hills."[5] With its mature trees and dirt paths, the campus reminded Jackie of the ranch.

Then near midday on September 17, 1923, Berkeley erupted in flames. A brush fire started in Wildcat Canyon, whipped down Codornices Canyon, crossed Cedar, and raced as far down as Shattuck Avenue. It seemed everything north of campus was on fire. The one o'clock classes had barely begun when the Campanile bells began to clang. Jackie remembers,

> *The hills went up in smoke. I can still smell it—hot, dry September air, tingling and ominous. . . . We wandered,*

> *scared and awed as refugees came down to our green campus lawns.*[6]
>
> *It was very exciting and very sad. The whole hill, you know, was smoking and burning behind them.*[7]

Phone lines were jammed and firefighters from San Francisco arrived by ferry. Jackie found Flo, and with four thousand student volunteers, made sandwiches for two thousand firefighters who fought into the night. Ben and Annie's daughter, Kerna Maybeck, rushed from her sorority to her childhood home. Dodging flames and the rifle cartridges exploding out of Wallen's dresser, she grabbed a few clothes and a satchel containing the deeds with one hand, and her frail grandmother, Blumie, with the other. In a letter to her mother, Kerna takes credit for saving a small Maybeck-built home across the street from her family home:

> *Muddie—*
>
> *It took me 10 min[utes] to get Blumie out, had to carry her, finally. Then I got the strong box, and got blankets for the boys to fight. . . . As soon as our house went, one boy and I got up on Mathewsons' roof with a hose—saved it. I carried furniture like a piano mover—Don't know where I got the strength. . . . I don't think I ever went through so much hell in my life.*
>
> *It must have been awful for Bud [Wallen]. He called from S.F. and got an incoherent answer. Had to come all the way over not knowing and just imagining.*[8]

Jackie heard from Wallen that evening; he and Bernard Maybeck had been working in San Francisco, and were indeed unaware of the fire until their return trip on the five o'clock commuter ferry. Their grand home, along with five hundred others in Berkeley, had burned to the ground; they were left with the clothes they stood in. Jackie and Flo's boarding house had survived. They walked up to La Loma the next day and gazed in disbelief at the twisted ruins, gas jets still burning amidst the rubble—there was so much destruction.

One can only imagine how the Maybecks felt. Now aged sixty-one, Bernard Maybeck had already suffered the loss of his office in the post-earthquake fire of 1906, and his monumental Hearst Hall on the UC campus had burned down in 1922. Now, his beloved Hillside Club and more than fifteen homes he had designed were lost in this 1923 fire. Wallen and his parents moved into an apartment down the hill. They were among four thousand persons rendered homeless by the fire.

Just prior to the catastrophe in the hills, Mira Abbott Maclay had published an article titled "The Maybeck One-Room House."[9] The piece reveals that even before the fire, when Maybeck's own home was huge and opulent, he was thinking small. He dreamed of compact hillside houses that merged the house with the garden, with several doors opening to the outside, and one large main room with wall beds that could open either inside or outside the room, thus providing for inside or outdoor sleeping, according to the weather. The dining room table could be put on wheels to allow cozy meals by the hearth or alfresco, in the garden. The kitchen should be in an alcove, equipped with the best laborsaving devices; the bath and closets were considered incidental. Maclay's article offered a preview of a new generation of Maybeck's family homes.

Not long after the fire, Wallen, who loved to camp, walked up the hill with his sleeping bag and settled on the cement floor of what had been his workshop at the old home. Bernard, perhaps excited about testing his idea of small houses, sent up carpenters and built Wallen one large, beautiful room on the site. Being familiar with John Rice's invention of a concrete concoction called "bubblestone," Maybeck dipped gunny sacks in a colored mix and hung them over slats nailed to the studs of the house. The randomly draped material evoked aspects of wood shingles, stone, or stucco, but best of all, it was fireproof. They called the tiny house, completed in 1924, the Studio, or Sack House.

Meanwhile, college life resumed for Jackie and Flo. "Nothing, not even the horror of the fire, had any effect on the excitement of being a student at the University," reports Flo.[10] Jackie decided to get a teaching degree to give her a way to make a living, but she preferred her art classes. She would lunch on a milkshake and graham crackers, swish

The Studio, circa 1924.

Photograph courtesy of Maybeck family.

her long skirts across campus, or hike with Flo in the hills in their baggy hiking pants and middy blouses. There were big bonfires in the Greek Theater; and then, "occasionally" Jackie said, "you studied."[11]

Jackie contemplates her image and her relationship with Wallen:

> *Dates were very important. I soon learned that if you were pretty you need not do anything—if not, you had to be vivacious and entertaining. I had unthinking good health and a wide smile. I think I was also enterprising, generous, hard-working, romantic, selfish, and lazy. And under all the foam of a new life flowed the deep, steady stream of Wallen's friendship.*[12]
>
> *I guess I always knew in my heart I would marry Wallen, right from the time I first met him. But I also felt that I had to have a little experience in the meantime, and also sort of prove to myself that I could attract other men.*[13]

Seeking that experience, Flo and Jackie met admirers from India at the Cosmopolitan Club. "Mine offered to hang himself on our palm tree if I wasn't kind to him," Jackie writes.[14] The evening was a disaster, but she managed to get home intact.

Jackie's Dutch Aunt Anna lived in San Francisco and encouraged students to gather at her place for Sunday tea. Flo's description of the trip across the Bay illustrates how different life was in those days: "In sunshine or in fog, night or day, riding on the ferry was adventure. The Bay itself stretching in all directions was a challenge to the imagination. The

Golden Gate, not yet bridged, lured one's thoughts to the mysterious lands beyond the Pacific."[15]

As always, Jackie was enchanted with the seasons in her new town:

> *What was also wonderful was Berkeley Spring—the most unexpected and contrary Spring anywhere. Heavy rains and cold would fill the early part of January, and then came an unbelievable spell of warmth and sun—the Spring interlude like a Chopin waltz. Skies became innocent blue—narcissi flew into bloom—Japanese quince became rosy red on gnarly stems.*
>
> *And at the end of January the plum trees were a heaven of pink blossom among small bronze leaf shoots. It made a giddy party picture along the streets. Sunsuits came out and shirts came off, and then crash, it's cold and rainy for March.*[16]

Although she returned again and again to dreams of a future with Wallen, Jackie continued to meet her high school beau, Huntington Benson, during vacations at the ranch, achieving "the state of weightlessness . . . by much kissing."[17] In the summer of 1925, Huntington asked Jackie what she wanted to be. Her reply was prescient: "I said, well, I was going to be a legend."[18]

Jackie's youthful confidence no doubt came in part from her very competent mother, Helene, who often managed the isolated ranch alone, while Pieter traveled and worked. Although he depended on it, Jackie's father frequently challenged her mother's independence. Jackie wrote that her mother bought herself a little Dodge for the ranch, and drove it up there with Wallen's help. "My father didn't like change and would not speak to her for a week."[19] And when Jackie and her mother put up fences or built gates, her father would frequently tear them down when he got back from his work, exercising his Dutch authority. But Jackie had grown up on the ranch working side by side with the men and could wield an ax or tar a roof as well as they could. Her daughter, Sheila, shed light on how the women managed: "Jackie's mother and her grandmothers were strong Dutch women who quietly manipulated the men—absolutely. Little Grannie [Annie Maybeck], Ben's wife, was like that too."[20]

Helene van Huizen and "Topsy Dodge," 1929.

Photograph courtesy of Maybeck family.

During her college years, Jackie looked forward to vacations on the ranch as a balance to the adventure and uncertainty of college:

> *When the brothers met our train, we were home and driving up the deep rutted road, and college was way back there. At home were hot drinks and a glowing stove and homemade Christmas presents. They clutched at the heart with love. . . . We were totally alone at the end of our string bean road.*
>
> *Sunday we walked those three miles to chicken dinner at Effie's and Bob's. We ate and sang "On the Trail of the Lonesome Pine," washed dishes, and walked home through fallen leaves and frost smells and skunk smells. . . . The deep love of this place churned in my heart. The day ended in deep sleep under a pile of quilts.*[21]

Wallen and Kerna sometimes rode their horses, Blackie and Exy, all the way from Berkeley to the ranch, sleeping along the roadside during the four-day trip and stopping in Hopland at a barn dance. At the ranch, they all slept on the big deck of Piet's cabin—just off the main house—and showered outside, with views to the hills and canyon. "Summer slid away and we hastened back to Berkeley and autumn fog and trains and classes and parties and girls again."[22]

As classes continued for Jackie, the Maybecks were busy. With Wallen living in the hills, Bernard and Annie bought an abandoned real estate office, hauled it up the hill, and placed it on the old tennis court above Wallen's new Studio. Completed in 1926, the little building came to be called the Cottage. It had a living room and a cozy coffee alcove, the kitchen was half outside, and the sleeping porch had a roof but no sides. Jackie and her college friends were asked to help build it on weekends:

> *Cement and foam were mixed in an old washing machine, we dipped sacks and hung them on the outside walls, and achieved a sort of Hansel and Gretel cottage, all rounded edges. Everyone stepped all over everyone else. Mr. Maybeck gave orders, Mrs. Maybeck served her homemade bread.*[23]

Jackie seemed to enjoy working with the Maybecks, but perhaps she was also contemplating a future role for herself within Wallen's family. Mrs. Maybeck must have understood and approved of the relationship blooming between Jackie and her son. In the fall of 1926, she invited Jackie and her brother Piet, (who had come down from the ranch to go to college), to live in Wallen's Studio. The one-room building had grown, sprouting a bedroom, bath, and deck added for Kerna, and a new balcony for Wallen. But Kerna had departed for a job in New York, so Jackie had Kerna's room, while Wallen and Piet slept on a balcony on the other side of the main room. The arrangement sounds like a precursor to coed dorms.

Life on the Hill with the Maybecks competed with college studies. Jackie and Piet became part of the Maybeck work team. Jackie explained that the Maybecks "liked young people around—we would be car drivers, dishwashers and talkers."[24] Neither Ben nor Annie knew how to drive, so Piet drove the car to the Freemarket and Jackie followed Mrs. Maybeck with suitcases for fruits and vegetables. Flo remembered gathering at the Maybeck Studio. "It was a wonderful place for parties and dancing, with a huge fireplace and a smooth concrete

The Cottage, 1925. *Left to right:* Ben and Annie Maybeck, Jacomena and Wallen and others.

Photograph courtesy of Maybeck family.

floor which needed only a sprinkling of flake wax to make it perfect for the turns and swirls of the waltz and fox trot."[25]

The seasons with the Maybecks broadened Jackie's outlook:

> *These were halcyon days, though I've never seen a halcyon. Annie cooked her fantastic meals in her Cottage kitchen which was half outdoors. . . . Maybeck's elegance rose like a flower from the disarray of the Cottage. He wanted everything to be silver-plated and wanted time to talk. . . .*
>
> *By the fireplace romance flowered. The lovely days brought Wallen and me into closer companionship, sympathy, and love.*[26]

Jacomena and Wallen, 1926.

Photograph courtesy of Maybeck family.

In her memoir, Jackie was clear about her reasons for going to UC Berkeley: "I had come to college to get into the world. I mainly learned from those four years of college a way of life. A way of balancing work with pleasure, simplicity with beauty, love with the future."[27] Her college experience and her growing involvement with the Maybecks furthered her assimilation as a Californian; but she did not disappear into the proverbial American melting pot. A distinctive confidence in herself arose from her Dutch roots, her experience as an immigrant, and her evolution as a liberated, college-educated woman of the 1920s.

SUMMER

FULL TILT INTO LIFE

Jackie and Wallen were engaged at Glen Alpine in California's Sierra Nevada mountains, "under a lovely moon and stars. He had our ring made of a platinum plate with tiny diamonds for the moon and stars."[1] But she hid that ring along with the fact of their engagement, keeping their vow to marry in September a secret.

Jackie graduated from Cal with a BA and a teaching certificate in May 1927 and headed for the ranch. That summer, she had doubts on the subject of marriage: "Can I ever be a one-man woman?"[2] She had kept up a lively correspondence with past beaux, and copied out long passages from her current philosopher, H. A. von Keyserling, who advised that "women must know how to treat Eros as the canvas and how to let the threads shoot backwards and forwards till an exquisite pattern is formed." Wallen sent her a book, *The Man Nobody Knows*, underlining "to do the easy thing is to kill the soul." In early June, Jackie wrote, "I've got to swing my mind around on Wallen. He's my job, my adventure, and when I really feel sure of that, I'll marry him, even tho' it's only September. If not, he must wait."[3]

At the ranch, Jackie was distracted from her uncertainty, as life was easy and sunny. She sewed, rode horses, planted flowers from the woods in her garden, read with her mother, napped, and rode into town for supplies. She was given a gift of a feisty colt that bucked and kicked her as she worked for weeks to tame him.

Then she had "A Big Idea. I'll marry Wallen, thereby uniting our lands here, and we'll come here for summers as usual, with Dad and Mother and Wallen when he can come, and make it a dude ranch, a resting place of congenial, amusing people. I've a new dream and a new aim at last."[4] Clearly, Jackie was not ready to leave the ranch. She added, "Then I want to rebuild our big straight chair and make it more comfortable. I wish summer could go on forever."

In July 1927, Jackie made a decision. She and Flo took the train to Portland, where Flo would finish law school and Jackie would sell curtains at Meier and Frank's department store. That August, still pondering marriage, Jackie wrote a wonderfully candid and intimate letter to Wallen:

Wallen:
I got a bit tired of the run of utilitarian letters I was panning off to you so this shall be somewhat in the nature of a change.

Your faith in yourself is so sure, you're so eager for danger and go up against it and still you have somehow never suffered, never "hit the bottom." But I'm not afraid of that and Wallen, you'll get life because you're looking for it now and it will probably get you down and make you suffer—right—perhaps you'll suffer thru me—I don't even think that anymore altho I did at first. There's a most awful lot ahead but we'll have to take it together and be not afraid, what ever it may turn out to be.

I haven't a clear idea yet what I'll do down there—Because what I want most is "expressive activity"—the field somehow doesn't matter so much because I haven't any decided talent or interests outside of people, gardens, adventure, dogs, horses, and the ranch, traveling, stage-work and you!

You know I've always thought of marriage as a problem—a few people solved it, many started playing but made nothing but fouls and blunders either thru selfishness, mental dawdling, or ignorance of the rules of the game. Sure it's a challenge and you know the weight of convention and custom, of what the other fellow does is rather terrific. I feel it but somehow I stand outside.

Now your new tack—that is the physical and mental ideal of course—so seldom realized. Most married couples satiate themselves by that very gratification of sexual impulse you spoke of until their energy is sapped and their senses dulled. The man especially, seldom realizes that, in doing so, he pours out a force and energy which might otherwise go into his creative work, for mental as well as physical achievements. The actual satisfaction is only of value biologically if it produces wanted children. You're on the track all right.

Nice to be able to say or think or write down absolutely anything that comes to mind. If only we can keep that. God what a lot of mid-Victorians we still have in this world!

If you ever write me a love letter I'll probably heave it into the ocean for that salt bath you seem to think it would require. I refuse to treasure an old relic like that, I like a new relic every so often, please Mr.

I want you a lot tonight but maybe if I saw you coming I'd run and hide. I've lived with ideas so long now I wonder what a real man is like.
Yours, sometimes—Jacomena[5]

Jacomena, 1926.
Photograph courtesy of Maybeck family.

In September, after courting for sixteen years, Jackie and Wallen consummated their love. Jackie took a bus to Vancouver, British Columbia, Wallen drove the old Packard up, and they were married in a little Episcopal church:

We didn't tell our parents. My mother knew what I was doing. . . . Neither Wallen nor I wanted to stir up the Maybecks, because it would be like putting a stick in an ant nest.[6]

[I] became Jacomena Maybeck. That name is still music to my ears.[7]

This urge to leave the extended family—to celebrate their occasions privately—would be repeated many times in Jackie's married life. She valued her independence and frequently clashed with the forceful Annie Maybeck. In a 1980 interview for *Gifts of Age*, Jackie talked with my coauthor, Charlotte Painter, and me about her long and complicated relationship with "Little Grannie":

> *She was a little Scotch-Irish fighter, a spitfire! She buzzed like a mosquito. When I was first married, it was a life and death struggle—I felt that my personality was going to melt down into the Maybeck family and never be heard of again.*
>
> *I suddenly realized that I had the privilege of being myself, my own person, separate from them. I had to fight for it in myself because I'd been carefully trained to be very respectful of older people. And to suddenly feel that I had the right to not accept the burdens they were trying to push on me. That was a big battle I won and I've coasted on that ever since!*

Annie wouldn't let Jackie serve "dirty alcohol" until Jackie surprised herself by saying, "Look, we're going to have a party and serve drinks and you may come to it if you want to." She felt that Wallen was under Annie's thumb, wanting to keep the peace, and going along with whatever the family wanted:

> *And then I came along. I didn't think it was necessary for Wallen to get up out of his warm bed at 11:30 at night to go pick them up at the Hillside Club. But there were ways of not hurting their feelings—we'd just go out of town on those nights!*

[Annie] was always trying to lay down the law, and Wallen was beginning to make laws for himself. He believed the only sin was hurting other people. . . . That caused a division in their philosophies when we were first married.[8]

It is well-known in our neighborhood and by Maybeck family members that Jackie and Annie did not have an easy relationship. Jackie had never come up against a woman so opinionated and decisive; but she stood up to Annie, and Annie found that unusual.

After their private wedding, Wallen and Jackie honeymooned at the Empress Hotel in Victoria, camped their way down the coast via the ranch, and then headed back to Berkeley to live in the Studio with Piet, just next door to the senior Maybecks. As one might guess, the newlyweds went right to work altering the space:

Wallen sawed a stove in two and set it under the balcony stairs with the oven on top to make it fit. I cooked my first turkey there—Thanksgiving. . . . and once more—as in 1923—we were going ahead full tilt into life.[9]

Jackie often spent a week or two at the ranch while Wallen made the rigorous midnight drive to be with her on weekends. For her, these frequent trips were a necessary respite from the intense and close-knit Maybeck family. She needed time out, time alone, and time with her parents, especially her beloved mother.

Jackie's daughter, Cherry, generously shared the *Ranch Log* with me.[10] It chronicles the comings and goings of visitors to the ranch and provides a fascinating commentary

Left to right: Ben, Pieter, Piet, Annie, Helene, and Jacomena at the ranch, 1927.

Photograph courtesy of Maybeck family.

about the early years of Jackie's marriage, including handwritten notes and drawings over a nine-year period. It reveals, among other things, that although Jackie needed breathing room, she nevertheless hosted various combinations of Maybecks at the ranch. A tiny photo pasted on page one of the log shows Bernard (now affectionately called Ben by both sides of the family) and Annie gathered with Jackie's brother, Piet, and her parents for Christmas dinner. "This fairyland is becoming more and more unreal and shows the beautiful dreams of the people who live here,"wrote Ben.[11]

I can picture Jackie and Wallen huddled in the rain, escaping their parents, as he recites the final stanzas of his poem, *A Hunting Season Honeymoon*:

Never can tell about a girl when you meet her at teas in town!
Got to get her out in the woods with the rain a-pouring down.
But you cooked that porcupine today and more, you ate your share.
With plenty of saleratus it tastes a bit like bear.

And now I can grin across at you, as I wait for the deer, and grin
At the gun in your hand with the wedding ring, and the set of your stubborn chin.

Lying out on the runway, with cold rain soaking through
That's the kind of a fool I am—and, thank God, you're that kind, too![12]

Wallen Maybeck, 1927.
Photograph courtesy of Maybeck family.

Back in town, Kerna was coming home from New York and needed her room in the Studio. Jackie and Wallen fixed their eyes on the double garage built in 1926 to house Ben Maybeck's first Packard (pet-named Packy). Down a path from the Studio, the garage was a long, low building, about eighty feet by twenty feet with wide overhanging eaves. Jackie and Wallen began remodeling it, adding a bathroom and a kitchen under the eaves and dividing the long room into a living area and a sleeping area. They called it the Cubby House.

The Cubby House; built 1926, addition in 1930.

Drawing by Sheila Bathurst.

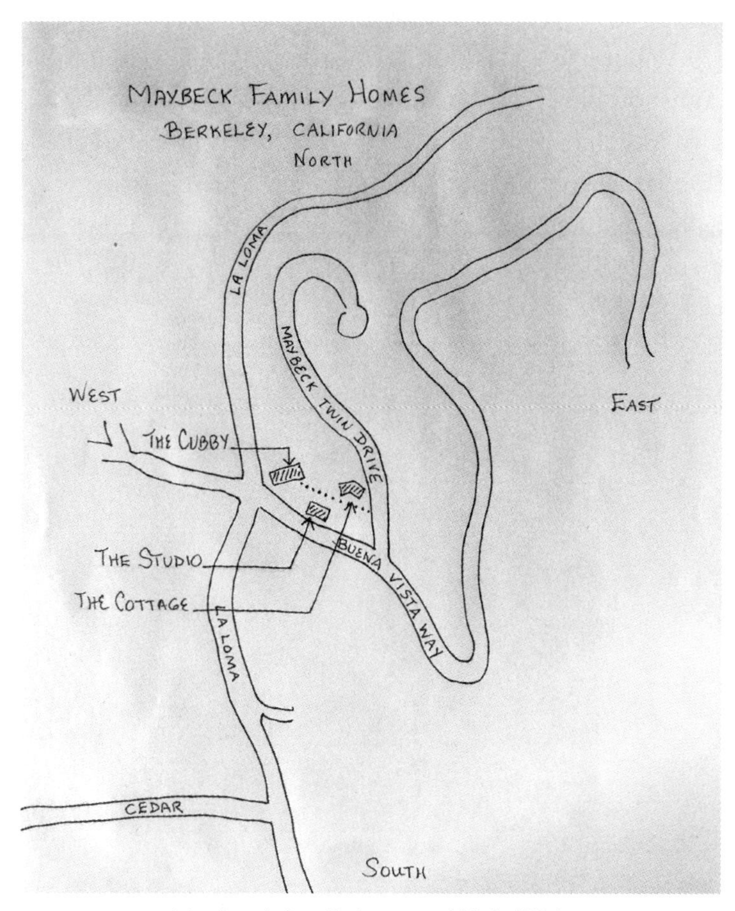

Maybeck family homes, 1924–1926.

Drawing by Pam Valois.

In the first year of her marriage, Jackie was surprised to find she was pregnant: "I was very absorbed in my own predicament and how I was going to handle it. Where we could go. I didn't want to have the baby here."[13] So again seeking privacy, she and Wallen left Berkeley to live on their own in Marin County, across the Bay.

While living in Marin, Jackie received a long letter from Annie offering help, but advising, "If you want to do it your own way and all yourselves, that's your privilege." She added, "One time you will not wish you were a man is when your baby is taking its meal—not out of a bottle. . . . I do wish you will be able to nurse it. It is the greatest adventure."[14]

Jacomena, 1928.

Photograph courtesy of Maybeck family.

On March 10, 1929, Adriana De Graf Maybeck (called Cherry) and Sheila Kern Maybeck were born in Ross, California. In a wire sent to Ben and Annie, then working in Los Angeles, Wallen wrote, "We had twins!! Two for the price of one!"[15] Ben answered, "Hurrah, stop, hurrah, stop, hurrah, stop."[16] Wallen's sister, Kerna, sent a rambling two-page letter to the hospital:

> *Hooray, I am absolutely flabbergasted! . . . You know when two people you care most awfully for have something wonderful happen to them it rather throws you into something like doddering idiocy. . . . Yes, Jac, you sure threw a bomb into the midst of several very sane households, and the result is havoc.*
>
> *Aunt Kerna (my god!!).*[17]

Wallen and the twins at the Cottage, 1929.

Photograph courtesy of Maybeck family.

But the telegram's exultations did not tell the whole story. Jackie, Wallen, and the doctor had expected one baby; instead, they were shocked as baby Sheila followed Cherry into the world. In a recent conversation, Cherry told me she feels that Jackie suffered a nervous breakdown, "became unlatched," after the births.[18] For the spirited and independent Jacomena, life turned upside down. She had no career, depended on the senior Maybecks for housing, and was confronted with giving up her old self for motherhood. She had not had a chance to develop the "expressive activity" she'd hoped for in her letter to Wallen just before their marriage. From the letter's long list of interests—"people, gardens, adventure, dogs, horses, and the ranch, traveling, stagework and you"—children are notably absent.[19]

Sheila believes that Jackie experienced postpartum depression; but since it was unrecognized in those days, she dealt with it quietly and privately, without the support that might be available today. Overwhelmed, Jackie took the babies home to the ranch to be nurtured by her mother for much of that first year.

When the twins were six months old and Jackie was recuperating, her mother writes an animated note in the ranch log:

> *The gang arrived Saturday evening. Sunday saw a tremendous display of energy, a digging and delving and hauling rock. . . . Piet and Kerna hauled rock to edge the flower beds, the "men" left to hunt, and Lenoire and Jac dug potatoes and picked beans for dinner. The gold fish are happy, and the twins and all their diapers and olive oil and bottles are packed and ready for another three weeks in town fog.*[20]

The ranch on Pine Ridge Road, 1929.

Photograph courtesy of Maybeck family.

In the ranch log, there are frequent flashes of Wallen's sense of humor as he came and went over the year, returning to "bachelorism" in Berkeley while Jackie and the twins stayed at the ranch. As Wallen never wrote his memoirs, it is challenging to get a sense of him and his thoughts, but his drawings and notes in the ranch log reveal his playfulness. Jackie called him "a kidder . . . full of little quips or little jokes, and puns! . . . He made music, he sang."[21] Katherine Sorensen, Jackie's granddaughter, remembers him as "undemonstrative, but affectionate in a remote way, and always willing to teach or talk to the young kids."[22] Cherry portrays him as a "quiet person who never yelled, but of course, Jackie was the boss!"[23]

When the twins were four months old, the little family moved from their Marin County rental to the Cottage, which was then empty because Annie and Ben were working in Los Angeles. Kerna and Piet were living next door in the Studio. Wallen continued his work with the telephone company in San Francisco, and he and Jackie slowly fixed up the Cubby House on weekends. Jackie's description of the days in Berkeley is poignant:

> *We were sleeping in a little bedroom we made by closing in the porch behind the living room of the Cottage. Kerna would come up and we would sit in back where we had cleared a little bit of land. We'd bring the babies out there in their baskets . . . and read and talk and drink tea, nurse the babies.*[24]
>
> *I was exhausted and cried into the babies' bath. But we all sat in the sun and grew well and brown.*[25]

Ranch log, December 1929.

Courtesy of Maybeck family.

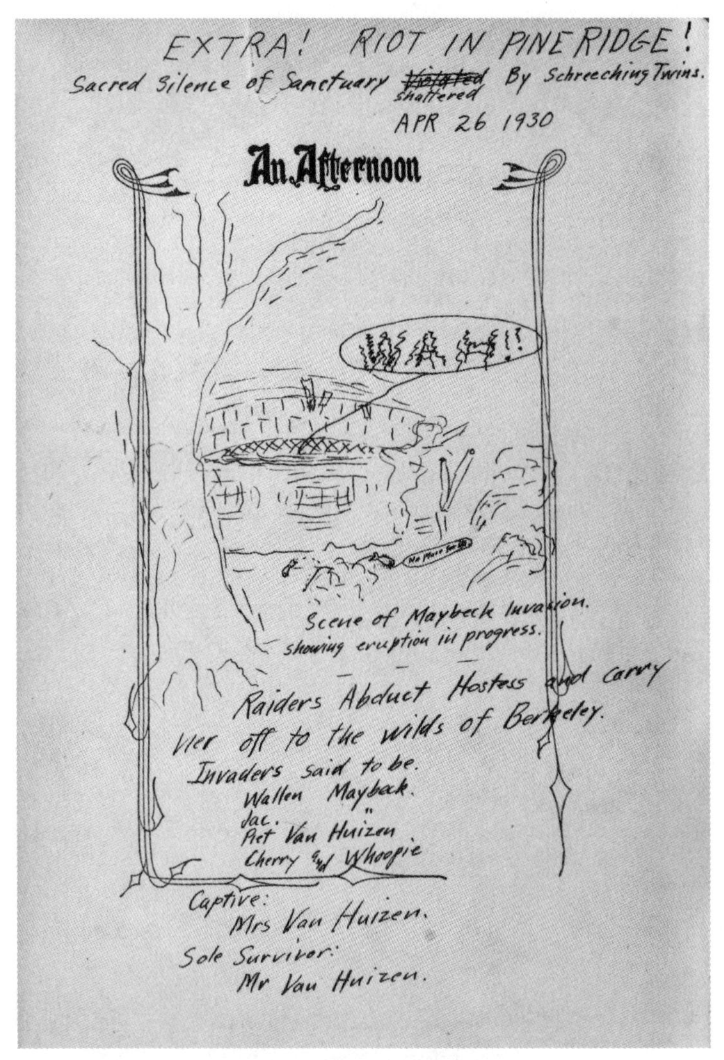

EXTRA! RIOT IN PINE RIDGE!

Sacred Silence of Sanctuary ~~Violated~~ shattered By Schreeching Twins.

APR 26 1930

An Afternoon

Scene of Maybeck Invasion.
showing eruption in progress.

Raiders Abduct Hostess and Carry
Her off to the wilds of Berkeley.

Invaders said to be.
Wallen Maybeck.
Jac. "
Piet Van Huizen
Cherry and Whoopie

Captive:
Mrs Van Huizen.

Sole Survivor:
Mr Van Huizen.

Ranch log, April 1930.

Courtesy of Maybeck family.

Jacomena with a twin at the Cottage, 1929.
Photograph courtesy of Maybeck family.

Kerna and Jackie remained close friends over their lifetimes. Kerna was an important confidant for Jackie, and a frequent guest at the ranch. She made a convenient ally for Jackie in that she adored her father, Ben, but did not get along well with her mother, Annie. After she and her husband, Chick Gannon, moved away from Berkeley, her letters to Jackie were filled with memories. "Like the time Haley's Comet was due to arrive and I wanted to put 'Tito' [the donkey] in the fireplace where he would be safe. I can hear Dad and Wallen consoling me that they couldn't get him up the stairs."[26] (The fireplaces in Maybeck houses are so big that a donkey could quite comfortably fit in one.)

Left to right: Wallen and pig, Annie and twin, Jacomena, Kerna and twin, Ben and Packy, n.d.

Photograph courtesy of Maybeck family.

Life with the twins unfolded while Jackie and Wallen worked to complete the Cubby House in time for Ben and Annie's return from Los Angeles to the Cottage, probably in the fall of 1929. In 1930, notes in the ranch log confirm that Jackie still counted on the comfort of the ranch: "April and flowers and the gray rain in-between, the twins have one worn down to a thin line but not too thin to enjoy this land of spring and the dear old woodticks. Back to town again for another month as the slave of society and then—summer!"[27] A note in August reads, "I woke up at 6 a.m. to find Aunty [Kerna] and Wallen sitting in the garden. Mother suggested that since I had slept all week, I should drive them to Berkeley. I stayed till Thursday being a social butterfly by night and at mealtimes, and a cement mixer by day."[28]

Packy in the mud, 1928.

Photograph courtesy of Maybeck family.

Jacomena and twins at the ranch, circa 1930.

Photograph courtesy of Maybeck family.

Ben, Annie, and twins on the ranch, 1930.

Photograph courtesy of Maybeck family.

Jackie and her family were now living in the Cubby House, but it still needed work: "Along about summer, we went up to the ranch, sunshine, and beautiful. But—while we were gone—Little Grannie built a long stairway and on top a fine bedroom, bath, dressing room and a sun deck. I wished I could have built it myself tho."[29] Jackie, in her inimitable way, added: "Much later, I put in a little fireplace to steady the place down, and also to block water from running into it."[30]

In November 1930, Showboat—a custom-ordered 1929 Dual Cowl Phaeton—was first mentioned in the ranch log. It was the second Packard given to Ben Maybeck as partial payment for his services, by the San Francisco automobile mogul Earle C. Anthony. "That big black cat of a car"[31] made the long trip to the ranch—a 120-mile drive north to Ukiah, then an hour's drive west over a dirt road—more comfortable, especially in the rain.

Researching the narrative of Jackie's life, I was puzzled by a note in the ranch log. In December 1930, she wrote: "The first time a Packy has made it to the house on Christmas. Next year the twins will be old enough to make the trip we hope. Beautiful weather and good company and fun."[32] This suggests that Jackie and Wallen were at the ranch for Christmas without the nearly two-year-old twins. Did the twins stay in Berkeley with the senior Maybecks or Kerna? Of course, neither Cherry nor Sheila remembers.

Although Showboat was now more desirable than Packy, Wallen wanted the family to keep both cars. In his large, scrawling handwriting, he sent a heartfelt letter to Annie Maybeck:

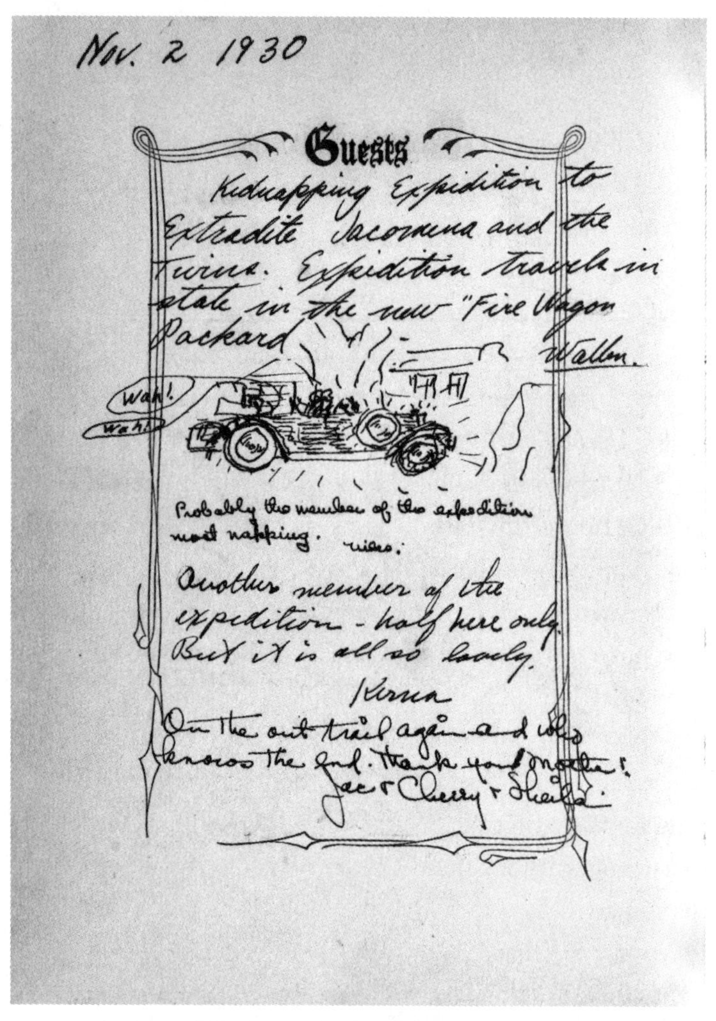
Nov. 2 1930

Guests

Kidnapping Expedition to Extradite Jacomena and the Twins. Expedition travels in state in the new "Fire Wagon Packard"

Wallen.

Probably the member of the expedition most napping. wies:

Another member of the expedition - half here only. But it is all so lovely.

Kerna

On the out trail again and who knows the end. Thank you Mother!

Jac & Cherry & Sheila.

Ranch log, November 1930.

Courtesy of Maybeck family.

Dear Ma:

I am afraid I will have to tell you on paper what my voice could not be trusted to explain.

I was sorry to force you to let me keep "Packy," because I know that is practically what I did. But I just did not have the heart to let her go. It just could not be done. That is all. And I know I never will be able to sell her. To every one else she is just a car. To me she is a friend. Practically every thing I have that means any thing at all to me is mixed up with that mess of metal. Without "Packy" those twins that have brought you so much real happiness probably would not even have got started. Love, Romance, Adventure, Beauty, Birth; You just can't sell those things.[33]

Wallen's comment about the twins is intriguing. Did he mean the car gave him and Jackie the means to escape into their own space—or perhaps even that the twins were conceived on the comfortable leather seats? In any event, Wallen did keep Packy, and in the 1940s, he and Jackie drove her across the country.

A priceless letter from Jackie to her mother provides a glimpse of life in the Cubby with twins:

Today, after I'd gotten them down for a nap, they took off their clothes and threw them out of the window into the plum tree. Then poor Cherry got a nosebleed and wiped it off on the window curtains. I guess they fell out of their crib because when I checked on them they were in my bed.

We took a walk and went into Grandma's house for a few minutes. They got into her flower box and pulled handfuls of ivy. While I was putting back the ivy, they opened the flour drawer in the kitchen and sprinkled it on the floor. They were so cute about wanting to help me sweep it up. Well anyway, they are asleep now and I'm a little tired—I could talk about them forever. Love, Jac.[34]

That summer on the ranch, Jackie wrote to the senior Maybecks,

I asked Cherry, "you're a sweetheart, aren't you?" "No, me's a Maybeck," she replied. Sheila is swinging a kitten by its neck like a dumbbell, one in each hand—she's almost never without a kitty. And so it goes. It's so dry and barren that the deer are desperate and have started breaking thru the orchard fence. These last dead days before the early fall change comes are pretty bad. Tempers and nerves get rather frazzled and we feel like Kansas farmers looking for rain. Languidly, Jac.

P.S. The kitten crop has decreased from seven to two.[35]

Back in Berkeley, Kerna had started calling Ben and Annie "the Family." With their houses now so close together, it seemed just right to the twins, as they frequently ran up the dirt path from the Cubby House to the Cottage. Wallen built a primitive baby monitor strung between the two houses, and called it the "Whoop detector," after baby Sheila's nickname, Whoopie. Now Jackie could sleep in, or she and Wallen could visit the Family in the evenings, leaving the twins at home. Cherry wrote:

Our parents built a six-foot chicken-wire fence to surround the deck off our bedroom and keep us from wandering, but our agile toes easily climbed up and over and we followed a path to the Blue Carpet House where Ben and Little Grannie lived. We'd climb into bed with them and they rubbed our backs. Ben never talked down to us. . . . He loved pomp and circumstances and the Middle Ages. At holiday dinners, we wore gold crowns and velvet robes of beautiful colors.[36]

I asked Cherry about her relationship with Annie. "Little Grannie was not difficult with us. I just remember that she kept tying stockings around our eyes and sang us little songs so we would nap."[37] Sheila compared the two grandfathers:

Grandpa, on the ranch, never picked us up—he'd pat us on the head and say we were "good girls." But we were comfortable; that's all we knew. But Ben was affectionate with us. He'd take us on walks into town up at Twain Harte. He would put a piece of glass over a painting and we were told to paint it. He said we painted beautifully! He tried to teach us German in the thirties—with drawings and pictures and German words. It's heart tugging to see his work for two little girls.[38]

Cherry and Sheila still treasure their copies of the "Grandfather Letters," posted to them in 1933 from Elsah, Illinois, where Ben was working on plans for Principia College.[39]

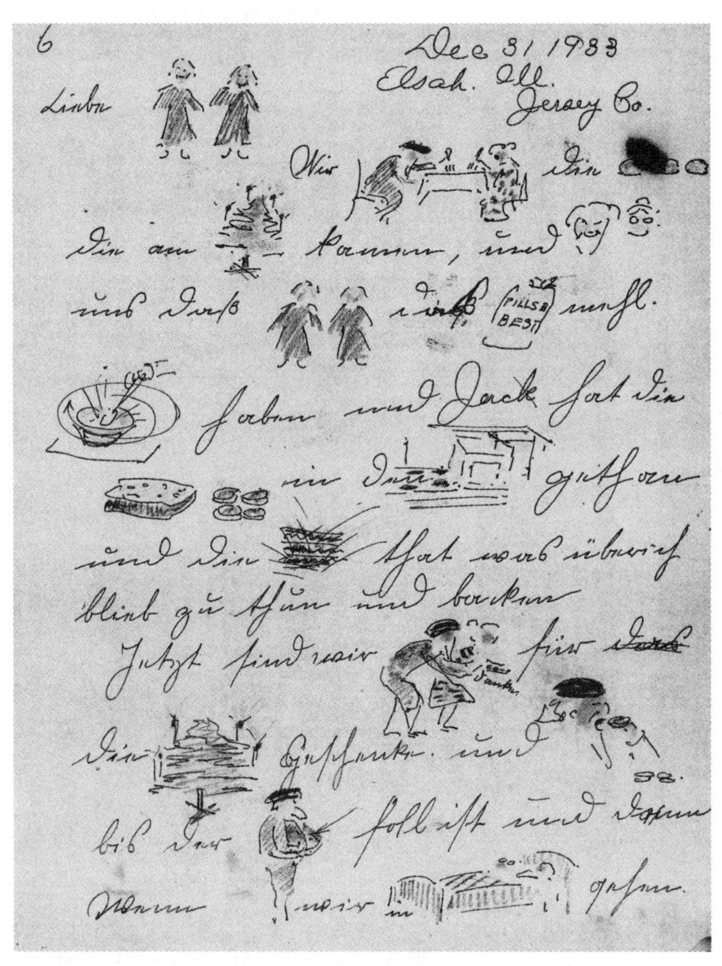

6 Dec 31 1933
Elsah. Ill.
Jersey Co.

Liebe

Wir die

die am kamen, und

und daß ich wohl.

haben und Jack hat die

in d gethan

und die that was übrig

blieb zu thun und backen

Jetzt sind wir für

die Geschenke. und

bis der voll ist und dann

wann wir in gehen.

Ben Maybeck's Grandfather Letters, 1933.

Drawings courtesy of Maybeck family.

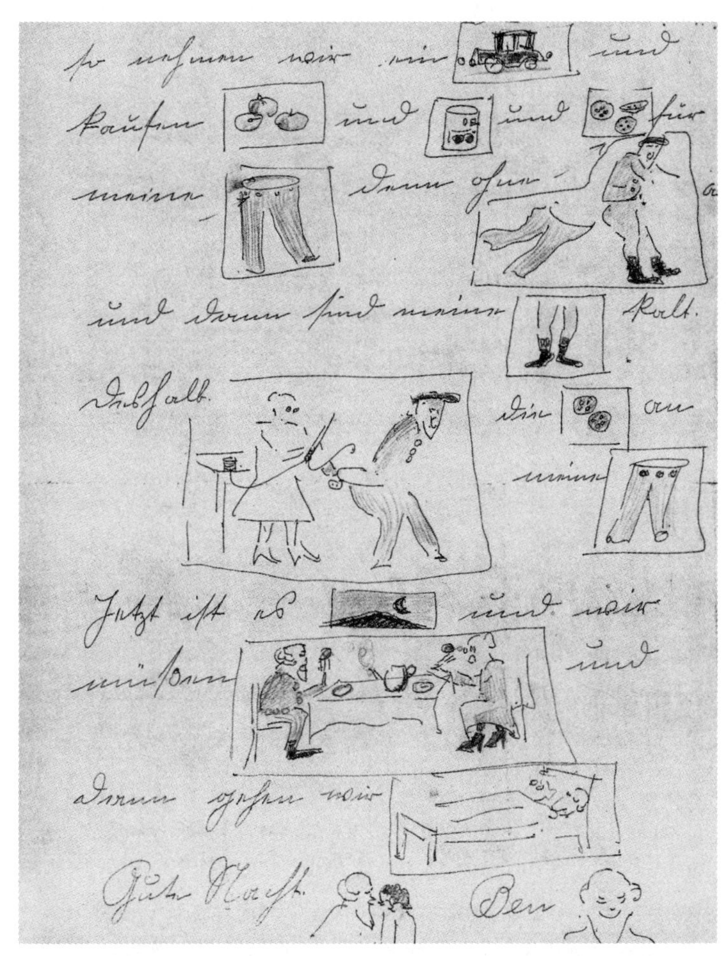
so nehmen wir ein und
kaufen und und für
meine denn ohne
und dann sind meine kalt.
deshalb die an
meine
Jetzt ist es und wir
müssen und
dann gehen wir
Gute Nacht. Ben

TRANSLATION: Dear twins, We are in a house in the country with mountains and a big river. Near our house is a school in which there are many children and also a chicken, a dog, and a cat. When we go to the store, we take a car and buy apples and cans and buttons for my pants because without buttons, I lose my pants and then my legs are cold. Therefore, my wife sews the buttons onto my pants. Now it is night and we have to eat dinner and then we go to bed. Good night. Kiss, Ben

As new homes were going up in the neighborhood around the Maybeck compound, Jackie found a kindred spirit in Ruth Pennell. She and her husband, Frank, had come from the Sierra foothills to raise their sons in a university community. In 1930, with informal sketches from Maybeck, they built a house on Buena Vista Way, across from the Studio. Frank was a carpenter and builder who would soon work on the house that would be built for Jackie and Wallen during the Depression. The Pennells' two young sons, Robin and Donn, grew up with the Maybeck twins. Robin remembers meeting the twins when they were "still on the bottle."[40]

Across the street from the Pennells, towering eucalyptus trees were cut down to make room for a new Maybeck project, the J. R. Tufts House. Completed in 1931 for the grand sum of $8,000, it was in Jackie's estimation "the most elegant and expensive house on the street."[41]

Long summer weeks at the ranch continued for Jackie and the growing twins, with sporadic visits by Wallen. The ranch was an ideal setting for the young twins. There were frequent visitors; Jackie could count on her mother's help; and it gave her a break from the senior Maybecks. Cherry and Sheila pushed their little wooden cart up and down the trails around the house and garden, trading places as driver and passenger. Jackie chopped wood for winter "in a shocking scant bathing suit to secure real freedom of action."[42] Sheila savored the mystery stories Big Grannie read to them: "The next chapter was highly anticipated the next day or even next summer. We were there every summer, reading books under a big oak tree."[43] Cherry describes the relaxed days at the ranch:

There was love and growth and time to study anthills, hear letters from Holland, and take cool evening walks. Jackie and Wallen slept in Piet's cabin and we were outside under the stars snuggled deep in our big double bed, jumping at a rustle in the oak leaves. They would sing a song, rub our back, and we'd fall asleep![44]

Piet's cabin on the ranch, 1931.

Drawing by Sheila Bathurst.

Twins in their double-decker chair, 1931.
Photograph courtesy of Maybeck family.

Wallen seemed extraordinarily tolerant of Jackie's need to be at the ranch. In September 1931, he wrote, "Married 4 years, been thru Reno twice and still the knot seems to hold. Shot off lots of ammunition and hit one peach and scared one skunk."[45] That October, he was optimistic: "Four months of bachelordom about to be terminated. Four months is a long time for me but fine for twins. May the summer have brought enough pleasant moments so that their memories will keep the next month bright."[46] Jackie was less enthusiastic about returning to Berkeley. She wrote to Kerna, "I've almost forgotten town and its habits and occupants. They have become vague nothings, just dim memories, a smile here, a tooth there, a blue dress, an earring, a cocktail, a burned-out cigarette."[47]

A HOME OF THEIR OWN

Back in town, the Great Depression had nearly brought residential construction to a halt. Just at this time, though, the senior Maybecks learned some wonderful news. Ben had been commissioned in 1923 to design plans for Principia College in rural St. Louis County, Missouri. But in 1930, before construction began, the city of St. Louis announced its intention to build a highway through the college property, and a new site had to be selected and designed. Principia became the biggest commission of Ben's career, allowing him to keep his San Francisco office open. Annie called it Ben's "pet baby,"[1] and Ben described it as "the chance of a lifetime. It has been given to few men to realize their greatest life dreams as it is being given to me."[2]

In 1932, Ben Maybeck found a way to keep his local staff and craftsmen working by designing two houses on Buena Vista Way in Berkeley. One was to be a home for Jackie, Wallen, and the twins, who were still squeezed into the Cubby House; the other was for himself and Annie and their daughter, Kerna. Twenty-seven-fifty-one Buena Vista Way (2751) was known as the Wallen and Jacomena

Maybeck House and also called High House by family members. Twenty-seven-eighty Buena Vista Way (2780) was known as the Kerna Maybeck Gannon House or the Annie Maybeck House.[3] Sheila explains, "We always called 2751 'High House' because it was just way up there on the side of a hill. It was wrapped around the hillside, with several doors opening onto gardens and decks. And of course, we named everything—the Studio, the Cottage, the Cubby House—and yes, the ranch was just the 'ranch.'"[4]

Wallen's and Kerna's houses were similar in plan, with differing orientations to the hillside. The application for a permit for 2751 Buena Vista Way, issued on August 1, 1932, states that the house was to be twenty-eight by forty-six feet, with a forty-five-degree pitch to the roof. The builder would be Philip Coats, and the estimated cost of the building was $3,000, including materials and labor.

Although Ben asked Jackie to help plan the new house, she recalled, "I was too awed by him to dare make any suggestions."[5] "I didn't know what the possibilities were. But I watched a lot and I learned a lot."[6] Later in life, Jackie created fictional cats that would have felt no such reticence: "If you want to know about a house, ask a cat," said one. "He knows where the sun comes in, where the cold side is, and where the ferns will grow."[7]

Ben's approach when designing a house was first to spend considerable time with his clients. He had told the Binghams, in Montecito, "I will design your new house if you will let me come visit your present home, to see how you now live, to listen to the music you like, and to learn what is important to you."[8] Of course, Ben knew Jackie and Wallen intimately, and the land and the house were a gift; they were not clients in the usual sense, although they may have helped pay for materials. I wonder what emotions Ben hoped to evoke in these special people as he sketched the spacious roofline with exposed trusses that draw the eye upward to the sky and trees. Perhaps this was his attempt to raise Jackie's spirits and to hold the family close.

Several principles may have guided the architect's thoughts in planning 2751. In 1906, Maybeck had helped produce a booklet for the Berkeley Hillside Club which was distributed to hillside lot buyers.[9] He wrote:

> *Hillside architecture is landscape gardening around a few rooms for use in case of rain—a dining porch on the southeast, a sleeping porch on the northeast, a play ground court on the east, and an observation porch on the west, but room to move and to breathe. . . . Build around the hill on contour lines or step the house up against the hill, one story above and back of the other. The correctly planned hillside house is parallel not perpendicular to the slope. It avoids the wind by hugging the hill, is firm and enduring because braced against it.*[10]

Ben admired the ideal described by his friend, Charles Keeler, in *The Simple Home*:

> *In the simple home all is quiet in effect, restrained in tone, yet natural and joyous in its frank use of unadorned material. Harmony of line and balance of proportion [are] not obscured by meaningless ornamentation; harmony of color is not marred by violent contrast. Much of the construction shows, and therefore good workmanship is required and the craft of the carpenter is restored to its old-time dignity.*[11]

Maybeck created elegant drawings for the Buena Vista Way projects on large sheets of crackly, thin paper. The final blueprints for 2751, dated July 1932, have bold notations enjoining builders to "LOOK AT ALL DRAWINGS" and scolding, "MISTAKE WAS MADE BECAUSE ALL DRAWINGS WERE NOT STUDIED BEFORE DECIDING ON MEASUREMENTS."

While plans for 2751 were being developed, Jackie and the twins spent the summer as usual at the ranch, enjoying weekend visits with Wallen and a special visit from Flo, who wrote: "A weekend at the ranch has so far stirred my domestic instincts that I shall bake some bread and buy a coffee grinder—here offering a prayer that the inspiration will last until Berkeley."[12]

Although the permit for 2751 is dated August 1, 1932, it is not known when construction actually began.[13] The ranch log and Jackie's diaries are unaccountably silent about the new house and its progress, nor does she speculate about a date for moving in. She must have been pleased as well as apprehensive, knowing that she would be expected to live in the house indefinitely—across from Annie and Ben in the Cottage—rather than settling elsewhere. And perhaps Jackie and Wallen could not quite believe they'd have a home of their own after so many years of shifting from one family house to another.

Pieter, Helene, and twins on the ranch, 1932.

Photograph courtesy of Maybeck family.

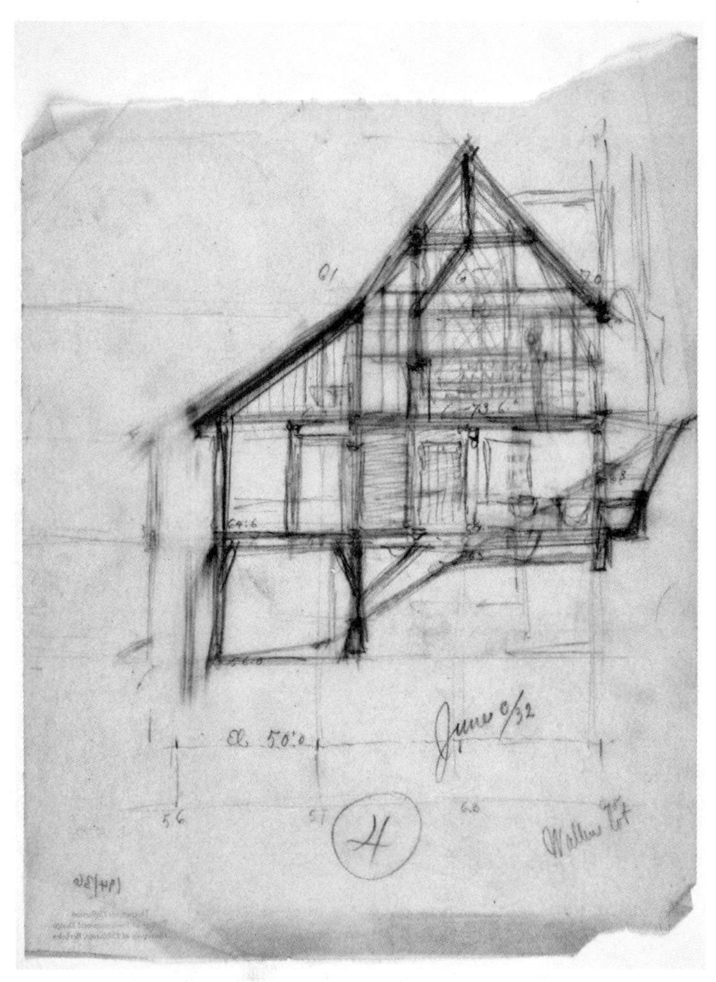

2751 Buena Vista Way drawing by Bernard Maybeck, June 1932.

Drawing courtesy of Environmental Design Archives, UC Berkeley, California.

Drawing of interior beams, Bernard Maybeck, n.d.

Drawing courtesy of Environmental Archives, UC Berkeley, California.

Ranch log, September 1932.

Courtesy of Maybeck family.

Twenty-seven-fifty-one Buena Vista Way began to take shape. The path to the house led up a dirt road (now Maybeck Twin Drive) via a rustic gate. Jackie wrote:

> *It has a slightly "Tobacco Road" look. For good reasons. It is strictly homemade out of scraps of redwood. It dates back to times when we made everything ourselves. But it succeeds in a look of welcome into the misty haphazard garden inside.*[14]

After following the winding path through the garden and up past an unfinished lower level—Wallen's workshop and a garage—a visitor came to a Dutch double door hung with oversized iron strap hinges. Cherry explains that you'd bang on a huge gong from India, rather than push a doorbell. "I'll always remember how fun it was to go down the stairs to the front door and open it for a date."

A small foyer with a floor furnace was welcoming, and if you looked up, you would see a hole in the ceiling which delivered heat to the kitchen upstairs through a grate. Handcrafted doors with inset glass windows led to three bedrooms with dramatically exposed framing. The twins' bedroom had graceful wooden arches over their little beds, and a tall fanlight window allowed Jackie to check on the twins from the deck above. Next to this bedroom, Annie Maybeck had the carpenters put an enclosed play space for the twins on the roof of the garage—a good idea for a house on a hill. In an earlier plan, the south bedroom (which would be Jackie and Wallen's) was to have a peaked roof, but Annie told Mr. Melvin, the master carpenter, "Don't waste space and sun."[15] So the roof was made flat and became a sundeck for the top level. It is not known whether Ben Maybeck challenged

Annie on this design, but an artifact of the original design, shingled like the roof, still rises partway to a point above the sundeck, hinting at where the roofline was to have been.

After a pause at the entrance in the modest downstairs foyer, family and friends climbed steep stairs for a special experience—one I am blessed to repeat often in the course of my days here.[16] As you climb the stairs, your eye is pulled upward by huge north-facing windows. At the top, you enter a great room, a combined living and dining area with dark herringbone flooring, maple-colored wooden walls, and Gothic roof trusses arcing over your head. A huge fireplace anchors the northeast end of the room. The narrow kitchen stretches across the south end, where ingenious deep swinging cupboards house pots and pans under a double kitchen sink. Matching banks of cathedral windows at each end of the great room offer a view straight up into the sky. Charles Duncan observed:

> *This aggregate space accommodated family interaction. One lived life in the Great Hall. Here one ate, talked, laughed, played, cried, sang, argued, and shared time with friends. Children were welcome in the adult world, and adults in turn could enter a forgotten childhood. . . . Maybeck's romantic translation of the great hall into the twentieth century promoted the family. It was this shared space that allowed the members to hold each other's interest in common.*[17]

French doors on the east wall of the great room led outside to an open porch, with space for an icebox, a tiny bathroom, and the washtub that Maybeck liked to place outside so the woman of the house could get fresh air. Cherry remembers an upright piano positioned next to the French doors, behind the stove:

> *Maybe we sang; Little Granny put a piano in every house and tried to get us to be musical, but we just weren't. But Wallen played the banjo and he was good at it!*
>
> *Dad was also very involved with the radio and the electrical world and installed special speakers so we could dance to Guy Lombardo and the other big bands. He had a collection of rifles in a glass-enclosed case at the bottom of the stairs but I don't think he hunted much.*[18]

The photo on page 80, although taken around 1950, shows the original configuration of the kitchen and the piano. The east (left) post of the truss was at some point enclosed in a cupboard; the hoodless stove was behind the cupboard in the far left of the photo. A small dining table sat at the south end of the room under one of the great windows. Jackie's granddaughter, Katherine Sorensen, now uses the table in her Seattle home, and reports that it can be expanded to nearly nine feet in length using the six leaves. Closet space at 2751 is scarce and seems to be made for small people with few possessions.

In 1976, Gerald Adams interviewed several owners of Maybeck homes and concluded, "Those who live in his houses cook, clean, sleep, entertain, heat and store their belongings in ways ordained by this genius." Jackie added, "Maybeck loved looking into the trees. He used to say, 'If you want to see the bay, walk up the road.'"[19]

2751 Buena Vista Way interior, circa 1950.

Photograph by Lionel T. Berryhill, courtesy of Maybeck family.

Jackie, Wallen, and the four-year-old twins moved into their new home in early 1933.[20] I was puzzled about the short time frame between the permit's approval in August 1932 and the move-in date. Anthony Bruce, director of the Berkeley Architectural Heritage Association, explains that Berkeley houses in the early thirties were, on average, built in just three months! The timing of Ben and Annie's move to their new house (2780 Buena Vista Way, sometimes called Kerna's House) is not well-documented. They probably moved in sometime in 1933, but then spent three months in the fall in Elsah, Illinois, on the Principia project, giving Jackie and Wallen a chance to settle into their new home alone.

2751 Buena Vista Way exterior, n.d.

Photograph courtesy of Maybeck family.

2751 Buena Vista Way, circa 1933.
Photograph courtesy of Maybeck family.

Jackie was pleased with High House: "Wow—a real house of our own!"[21] "We began to be much more presentable people . . . we had a good house. We could invite our friends up here."[22] With Flo, she planned an elegant housewarming with music from the radio coming from every direction, thanks to Wallen's hidden wiring. Flo, who called it the JacandWallen house,[23] wrote about the easy way friends gathered:

> *Eight was the right number for a sit-down dinner. There was still Prohibition . . . and for a proper dinner party, we needed liquor. We knew a young man who could get us drinking alcohol which we cut and flavored. . . . And I made a very respectable black fig wine. . . .*

The eight of us were our host and hostess, Wallen's sister Kerna and a charming young man she did not marry, our doctor friend Kay, another doctor named Hunt, a friend of Jacomena's from high school days, and I with a handsome young German who danced like a dream. The men wore their tuxedos and we our long dresses after the up and down hemlines of the Twenties.[24]

Cherry adds that she and Sheila would sneak upstairs early the next morning to see what was left out on the table, and "we'd taste the drinks!" I imagine that Annie disapproved of this glamorous lifestyle happening right next door. Flo continues her story:

Katia, a White Russian girl . . . borrowed the new house and sent out her invitations, instructing each guest to bring a sheet and pillowcase. Wallen and I were stationed at the front door and as each guest arrived, we directed them into the bedrooms where we helped them get wrapped into the sheets and cut eye holes in the pillow slips. At the top of the stairs . . . there was a large sign forbidding talking there. On the doors . . . were signs stating what WAS to be talked about in each place—philosophy, art, love. . . . At midnight, we unmasked and the dancing went on. If one hasn't danced with a Russian, one simply has not danced.

Those parties were the highlights but we had casual ones nearly every weekend, mostly at the new house which was so perfect for them. . . . We were all hikers and on the Friday or Saturday night of a full moon, we set off to walk in the hills, still wild and for the most

> *part without houses. . . . Every Sunday morning, we had breakfast at someone's place.*[25]

The stories about friendships and parties during these years paint a picture of a life of ease and pleasure, a world both natural and elegant.

It was the first year in their new home; yet Jackie, Wallen, and the twins spent Thanksgiving at the ranch and, hauling up a new stove, celebrated Christmas there too. In fact, the next eight Christmases were spent at the ranch. Jackie declared in the ranch log, "It is so good and real here."[26]

Real is an interesting word to describe what Jackie loved about the ranch. For her, it was a place where she felt free to be herself, and live a simpler life. There was no gap there between herself and her relationship with her mother, something she often missed feeling in Berkeley. Jackie recorded her private thoughts in her diary:

> *I enjoy myself a lot these days. That is—I am often a source of surprise and amazement to myself. I can never foretell just how the inside of me will react and suddenly find it excited or angry, delighted, or forlorn. That is amazing to the top layer of me, which I used to be afraid of—these moods—and loathe to examine them.*[27]

Jackie could relax into her mother's caring, get help with the twins, and work with her hands to form things from wood and stone. These ranch visits gave her faith in herself, and confidence that she would eventually find answers about work and who she was.

It was then 1934, and as the babies grew out of infancy and into two little toddlers, life in Berkeley got easier. Jackie could visit with her friends from university days who were getting married and having children. "The parties became much more subdued, much more family style."[28]

While Ben and Annie were frequently away in Illinois, they wrote voluminous letters to Kerna and Wallen, filled with news of the day and thoughts about everything from the meaning of Christmas cards to Roosevelt's next move. Annie's presence was ubiquitous, such as when she sent advice to Wallen urging him to "be a better Dad." She prefaced a twenty-four-page letter by saying, "I've got to release once in awhile or collapse":

> *Those babies are growing up—they need you. Jac thinks you want society so while you are home she lets the twins go. But there really is a reason why children often have two parents. Frank Pennell is a country boy but he reads to his boys for 20 minutes after they go to bed, regular service. Ruth is a scatterbrain, but she has a house full of children's books and takes her boys over to the University to bird and animal exhibits. Sheila and Cherry can't make "S and C" any better than a year ago. They should speak German now if you'd been on your job. . . . I read little things between the lines—why, this and that—and that Cherry kicks a window in, why? In many ways, Jac is a wonderful mother. But there must be a reason why I have several times heard, "Wallen does not know that he has any children." I am a strong believer in "what is right."*[29]

Annie was also vexed that Jackie wanted curtains in the new house for privacy, adding,

> *So we put 2751 with windows so big and such a shape we thot [sic] no one could afford to curtain them and with views so gorgeous no one in his senses would shut them. . . . I even made the sleeping porch at awful expenses of time and thot and money so no one could see in.*

I have found nothing from Wallen suggesting how he actually felt about this withering criticism from his mother. But judging from his outward life with Jackie, he seems to have taken it in stride. He and Jackie took walks "and talked long and hard."[30] Showboat carried them around at night to parties and dances and the nearby Hillside Club. "We wore evening dresses with gardenias on our shoulders and the men wore tuxedos. Daytimes we wore sun suits and worked in the yard. It was strange for Ben," Jackie writes, "who liked his ladies elegant, to see us setting fence posts and building stone walls."[31]

Sheila remembers a joyful childhood. "There was a fort in the woods, classes at the Temple of the Wings with little costumes, and we loved to slide down the hills to the Drive on slices of cardboard."[32] She and Cherry played around houses under construction, discovering forbidden materials such as cans of paint. Their young neighbor, Robin Pennell, adored the twins, claiming he could tell them apart. Robin, who still lives in the neighborhood, told me about life on the hill in those days, painting a picture of a bygone style of childhood in the Berkeley hills:

Kids came up here because it was sort of a wild area—we had such freedom. Some of the girls had little playhouses complete with fireplaces but my father built us a "ship" that hung from cables, about ten feet from the ground. You had to climb a ladder to get to it and then you swung back and forth between our house and Kerna's.[33]

The kids loved to see the iceman arrive, chipping chunks of ice for a treat. And everyone knew the unique sound of each car as it chugged up the hill. Neighbors gathered frequently:

Somebody would say "come by" and the next thing you'd know they'd say, "what are you having for dinner—why don't we have dinner together?" Then somebody would bring a salad and pick up a few more people and the next thing, there'd be a party going on.

Children weren't excluded—I remember dancing with Jacomena when I was twelve or thirteen years old. She loved to dance and was always out there on the floor. I'm telling you it was like dancing with no one in your arms—she was so light, such a wonderful dancer. I have to say, in a lifetime myself, that the three best dancers I've danced with are Jacomena, Cherry, and Sheila.[34]

Sheila's memories of her mother during her childhood are nuanced:

We liked her, were happy with her. She would stretch out on her couch reading a book or magazine; she didn't pick us up and hold us on her lap but we could climb onto the couch and she would rub our feet. That was being

> *affectionate. She'd put us to bed and say prayers with us but not sort of "I love you," and no cuddling and kissing and that kind of thing—she just sort of let us be.*[35]

Was Jackie still depressed, or perhaps, overwhelmed? In a photo taken on the twins' fifth birthday—the only photo found of the family in 2751—she looks melancholy as she gazes away from the camera. Or was she feeling thwarted after reading one of her mother-in-law's letters to Wallen? If so, Jackie might have felt she couldn't even order curtains, much less put a stamp of her own on her new house.

In April 1935, Jackie fell ill with a serious form of tonsillitis, and could neither speak nor swallow for a week. Her mother cared for her in Berkeley for five weeks, and when Jackie was well enough, the two of them and the twins retreated to the ranch. Cherry and Sheila finished kindergarten at the Pine Ridge school where Jackie had taught after high school, and their visit lingered into the summer.

Jacomena, Wallen, the twins,
and Kerna Maybeck, March 1934.
Photograph courtesy of Maybeck family.

In November, her mother wrote, "Beautiful ending of a long, pleasant summer in which much hammering and sawing was done by Jac, resulting in a couple of good looking chairs and other improvements in the kitchen."[36] Jackie wrote in her diary,

> *It's hot as a griddle. We wear almost no clothes and sweat and sweat! I love it but poor mother wilts. I feel my town self melting away and leaving my old self whose main interests are twins, gardens, and family—I can't possibly be a real relative of the dancing lady known by the same name in town.*[37]

Jacomena at the ranch, n.d..

Photograph courtesy of Maybeck family.

This time, Jackie's sojourn away from Berkeley had lasted six months. She, Wallen, and the twins returned to the ranch for Christmas, then planned a move back to Marin County rather than return to their High House.

It seems surprising that Jackie would want to leave her new house after just three years. Significantly, though, Annie and Ben were back from their long trips to Elsah, Illinois, because Ben's work at Principia was largely finished. Jackie explained in her memoir, "When the twins were in the first grade we decided we wanted to get away from just the family all the time. You know, this was a very in-grown family—all these members, everybody depending on each other, seeing each other all the time, carrying around each other's packages."[38] Sheila adds, "It was too clobbering, too close, with the Family. Jackie was a powerful person and did not like to be constantly monitored and asked questions. So again, we changed schools and houses and moved to Ross."[39]

In an unpublished essay, Jackie wrote that they had left their modern High House with its luxurious gas furnace for "a year of freedom in this draughty old house across the Bay in Marin County because we wanted a change. You'd think we'd be ashamed but we are not."[40]

In the sunny little town of Ross, Jackie was inspired to paint and write, "nothing worthwhile, but I did it, because I just wanted to express myself."[41] With the twins finally in school, she was content: "I was left to my own devices. I did a lot of gardening . . . pulling weeds and making it look nice, and just enjoying myself, *my* house and *my* garden [italics added]."[42] Among the weeds, Jackie found, if only temporarily, something she'd long searched for—a means of expression that felt like her own.

Jackie's enthusiasm reminds me of our discussions in the 1980s when she and I talked about the challenge of pursuing creative work while mothering young children. We agreed with Tillie Olsen, whose recent book, *Silences*, was giving voice to those of us struggling with the issue:

> *In motherhood, as it is structured, circumstances for sustained creation are almost impossible. Not because the capacities to create no longer exist, or the need (though for a while as in any fullness of life the need may be obscured), but . . . the need cannot be first. It can have at best only part self, part time. . . . Motherhood means instantly interruptible, responsive, responsible.*[43]

With young boys at home, I had created a makeshift darkroom, hauling chemicals up a narrow staircase to the attic. Jackie encouraged me to make time for creative work, wisely suggesting that I hire a babysitter for one morning a week so I could work on photography. Everything had to happen in those three hours, regardless of the light or how I felt that day. As described elsewhere in this book, besides sitting for her own portrait, Jackie helped arrange meetings with her friends for photos that would become part of my exhibit and book, *Gifts of Age*.

ANOTHER HOUSE, ANOTHER FIRE

With Jackie, Wallen, and the twins living happily in Ross in the mid-1930s, Ben and Annie decided to move into High House themselves, as it was sitting empty. They quickly settled in, placing Ben's huge drafting table right in the middle of the great room. Jackie's feeling that the house had never really been hers to begin with deepened. She must have longed for a home of her own—one that she could count on in the same way she counted on the ranch. In the decade since her wedding, life had been so busy and unsettled that she did her best to create "home" wherever she landed with those she loved—Wallen and the twins, or on the ranch with her beloved mother.

Unfortunately, after Jackie and her family had lived in the Ross house for a year or so, its owner broke his leg and, as a result, needed his house back immediately. In her book, *Maybeck: The Family View,* Jackie bluntly summed up the situation: "We wanted to come home, but the Family did not want to move again."[1]

> *So we came home and said, "What are we going to do? We need our house," 2751, because the family always said that was our house. "We really want our house back. What are we going to do?"*[2]

I asked Jackie's daughter, Cherry, how her parents felt about being barred by the senior Maybecks from returning to what they believed to be their own place. She told me, "Jackie and Wallen didn't accept it—they would talk around it and figured that there might be another spot for Ben and Granny to go, but it just didn't happen."[3] Sheila also explained that Wallen wasn't really a fighter, and reminded me that Jackie and Wallen had occupied Ben and Annie's home, the Cottage, while the senior Maybecks were in Los Angeles. The implication seemed to be that as an outsider, Jackie didn't easily accommodate to the Maybecks' fluid sense of place and property, and that no matter what the paperwork said, things would be (and mostly were) owned by a third entity, the Family. Even though the Cottage and Studio were then rented to students, the Maybecks did not ask them to leave; and Jackie and Wallen did not insist on moving back to one or the other.

In any event, the Family solved the problem in classic Maybeck form: they gave Jackie and Wallen a piece of land and built them another house—this one on a windy hilltop on Purdue Avenue, Kensington, about three miles away from 2751. Cherry remembers, "It was an exciting lot! It was a big happening and a fun house."[4] During construction, the Wallen Maybecks rented an apartment on Solano Avenue in Berkeley and the twins attended yet another school. Jackie's poster-size drawing on page 95 shows the long and winding road the little family had traveled.

Jackie wrote, "There does not seem to be any good reason why this shouldn't be home tho' it's over a butcher shop! We're so glad we got ourselves out of the ranch before winter mired us completely. We are grateful for any place to lay our heads tho' it's on a lamb chop."[5] She could see the skyline profile of her new house from the kitchenette window in the Solano apartment. She dreamed of it being finished, confiding to her diary that "my dear dream almost died of anemia this summer—I went to the house today; there it was, two rooms and a bath like a set of sad old ruins."[6] Secretly though, she'd saved up enough money to buy Wallen a bathtub for Christmas, calling the gift a triumph.

While planning the Purdue house, Ben got books from the library about English manor houses and fireplaces, and Jackie and Wallen picked the ones they liked best. Living amongst a family of builders brought gifts and challenges; perhaps this new Maybeck house would finally be their own. The fireplace was huge, with a Venturi chimney, a feature of many Maybeck houses, and the building was constructed of concrete and steel so it would not burn. Jackie wrote, "It was a concrete monolith with a forty-mile view. Really kind of great if you could stand up in the wind."[7] Again, Jackie and Wallen did much of the building themselves. They called the house Hilltop and though it was only half-finished, moved in on New Year's Day, 1938. Wallen would later comment, "Shoemakers' children go barefooted. I have spent most of my life in unfinished houses."[8] Cherry remembers Jackie being satisfied with the house, as it was a good distance from the Maybeck compound in Berkeley. She then quickly adds that she really doesn't remember what Jackie thought, because "Sheila and I were unappreciative of our mom in those days and probably didn't care what she thought."[9]

Jacomena's homes, 1937.

Drawing by Jacomena Maybeck, courtesy of Maybeck family.

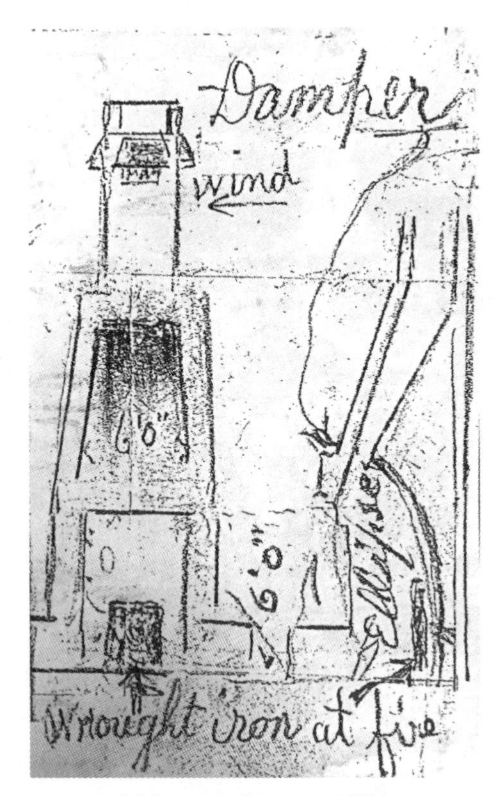

A Venturi chimney, 1956.

Drawing by Bernard Maybeck, courtesy of Maybeck family.

Jackie, herself, was becoming a builder of unusual and beautiful houses:

> *I worked like a pioneer woman all day and got such coal dust on my hands as would barely come off. House building is more than just rushing ahead doggedly; one must stop and rest and dream and re-visualize the house and the life one is working toward. The wind roars and I don't mind—I love it—it's mine and tho' still an ugly unfinished duckling, we swell with love of it.*[10]

Twins at Hilltop, 1940.

Photograph courtesy of Maybeck family.

Hilltop Christmas card, 1938.

Drawing by Jacomena Maybeck, courtesy of Maybeck family.

There was also a large piece of land to develop at Hilltop. Jackie's diary in early 1938 is filled with detailed plans and sketches for the gardens and pathways. "I grow dizzy with all the things I want to do." She moved in time and rhythm with the days and the seasons, criticizing the pansies and roses for blooming in December: "It seems a little tactless—I do like flowers that stick to their seasons."[11]

The twins loved the house, saying the big yard at Hilltop smelled like the ranch in the summer. They easily made friends at their new school. And because it was several miles from the Family, Jackie could "sit with my back to the warm stone of the house and just look and dream."[12]

After they had moved into Hilltop, Jackie tersely recorded a momentous family event in her diary: "Mrs. M. had her fire at 2751."[13] Back at High House, Annie had been frying potatoes for lunch and left a pan of grease simmering on the stove while she and Ben went down the hill on a quick shopping trip to get ingredients for the lunch she was making for her helpers. High House erupted in flames. Our neighbor, Robin Pennell, then ten years old, vividly recalls seeing clouds of smoke rising from the rooftop as he raced home to call the fire department. Richard Ward was seventeen at the time, working for the Maybecks as an all-round helper and driver, and living in the south bedroom. He remembers that when the three of them returned, Annie "ran up to the kitchen door to use the garden hose, but I had taken it down for washing the car and hadn't brought it back. She chewed me out on the spot—with the house burning inside."[14] The *Berkeley Daily Gazette* of that evening

(October 15, 1938) reported, "Smashing out a window pane with her bare hand in order to let the smoke out, Mrs. Maybeck assisted her husband in attempting to combat the flames until the fire apparatus arrived."[15] Firemen chopped a hole in the peaked roof and flooded the house with water. Windowpanes were blown out, their steel frames warped with the heat; the honey-colored maple floors were badly blackened; yet the tall beams remained intact. The wood was charred to the bottom of the stairs. But the bedrooms and bathroom were left untouched.

Annie remarked wryly, "At least this saves me a disagreeable job I had planned for tomorrow . . . to clean out the black widow spiders that have been over-running the place."[16] Asked why she thought Annie was smiling in the photo taken soon after the fire, Sheila said, "Little Grannie liked things happening—things that were challenging and that she could manage."[17] But seeing the ruin of her former home, Jackie called it a dreadful mess.

Annie Maybeck convinced the insurance company to give them money to restore the house themselves. Richard Ward "spent all of my spare time the next school year up on the scaffolding, lining the charred, knotty white pine ceiling with newly stained plywood and coving."[18] He moved over to the Cottage with his friend, Horace Fritz, during the reconstruction and describes sleeping on the bunk beds in the outdoor sleeping porch: "Fritz slept on the top, and me on the bottom. It was about the coldest and wettest environment we ever lived in. The Berkeley fog rolled in every night, and the bedding was forever wet."[19]

Ben, then in his late seventies, strapped on his tools and climbed the scaffolding, startling Richard with his vigor. Ben had used a version of the Japanese technique *shou-sugi-ban*—in which wood is deliberately charred and scored—in many of his houses. Then he sandblasted the interior of 2751, creating beams and trim that shimmered in the light.[20]

Ben and Annie with the twins, post-fire at 2751, 1938.

Photograph courtesy of Maybeck family.

FOLLOWING DADDY

Jackie and her family lived in their Hilltop home for just four years, never to return. War came in 1941, and Wallen was called to active duty in the Army Signal Corps to serve with the Army Air Corps. He had been a sharpshooter in the ROTC at UC Berkeley, using his skills to shoot flu medicine bottles off a fence.

Since marrying in 1927, the couple had lived in eight houses—the Studio, the Cottage, the Cubby, two Marin rentals, High House, the Solano Avenue apartment, and finally, Hilltop. A house was built especially for their young family, and then taken away. I recall Jackie saying, "I'm used to change—I've lived in some very funny places. You can slide through anything and don't feel upset by it." A childhood in Java and Holland and several moves around California had taught Jackie not to rely on sameness and continuity for a sense of security. Beyond knowing how to live with change, Jackie seemed to promote it, escaping to Marin County and the ranch. Wallen accepted this quality in his partner, and perhaps shared it. He had seen his childhood house burn to the ground, and made do with fluctuating living quarters since then.

Wallen Maybeck, Army ROTC, 1918.

Photograph courtesy of Maybeck family.

Wallen Maybeck, Army Air Corps, 1941.

Photograph courtesy of Maybeck family.

With the outbreak of the war, the family was on the move again. For the next two years, Jackie would make a home for her family in army facilities. She and the nearly teenaged twins joined Wallen in February 1942, at Hamilton Field near Novato, California. Sheila remembers being unfazed by the journey: "We just went where the parents went—they were cheerful about the moves. We got to walk to the PX and the soldiers whistled at us. Daddy got the measles and was very sick but we loved dancing with the young soldiers."[1] Cherry confirms, "We had no worries about the war—we just followed Daddy in our old Packy."[2] When Wallen was transferred, the twins moved in with a colonel's family to finish junior high school while Jackie retreated to the ranch.

Eventually, Wallen was assigned to New Mexico, where the family rejoined him. Jackie fell in love with the small town of Alamogordo: "We had never seen this kind of country. Sun and wind and enormous skies, and those adobe houses."[3] For two years, they lived in a little four-room cottage that included cockroaches, but Jackie made good friends and "left with great regret."[4]

After the summer sunshine and dancing every night came snow and a "German, tight-up" community in Ohio.[5] Then it was on to New Jersey until Wallen was suddenly ordered to England, where he served as a cryptology officer, a job critical to wartime intelligence and one shrouded in official secrecy. At this point, Jackie and the twins were tired of moving, and she felt the girls needed a home of their own after attending six different schools in two years. While Wallen flew to London and "experienced Buzz Bombs,"[6] Jackie taught the fifteen-year-old twins how to drive old Packy, and they headed back to California, picking up soldiers on the way. Cherry remembers that she and Sheila were "now on a different level with Mom—we were friends," and they started calling her Jackie.[7]

Left to right: Cherry, Jacomena, and Sheila in Ohio, 1944.
Photograph courtesy of Maybeck family.

I asked Cherry how Jackie had decided to return to High House instead of their Hilltop home. "I have no idea, but I do know that there was no distress."[8] Sheila added, "Jackie just said, 'We'll be going home and we'll need more furniture.'"[9] Cherry's son, Scott Nittler, thinks that Hilltop had been rented out, and the senior Maybecks had moved to their cabin in Twain Harte because their drivers—students living in the Cottage—had all enlisted. So, High House was standing empty! Jackie writes about the homecoming:

> *And of course Berkeley was a little foggy, and a little smelling of eucalyptus trees, and the house was absolutely desolate looking, inside. . . .*

> *. . . Our furniture was stored in Antioch. . . . We didn't get it back for a year.*[10]
>
> *It was a sad bedraggled house, sand still clinging to corners and broken glass in the garden.*[11]

While Wallen was serving in England and France, Jackie worked to put things in order again, grateful for a home for the twins who now attended Berkeley High School. She dusted the cobwebs, bought some furniture, and scraped the blackened, burned floor, using strong detergents. The floor stayed as it wanted to be, dark brown and mellow, some of it as textured as slip rock; "but fire and sand made an inexpensive pine house into a soft-colored, carved thing of beauty."[12]

Settling in, Jackie acquired a puppy named Tookie and enjoyed old friends. As more of the men came home, there were dances on the weekends. Sheila smiles, remembering the advice Robin Pennell gave her upon returning home:

> *Robin told us what to wear—it was as though we'd come back from outer space. "There is a hierarchy at school; if you want to be accepted, this is what you need to wear—sweaters, longish skirts, and only white socks."*
>
> *And no wonder they called it Nut Hill; everyone up here lived a little differently. We were kind of embarrassed about our house because it was so different from everyone else's house. We know they thought it was interesting but a bit strange.*[13]

No wonder indeed. There were Nobel laureates and visiting artists such as Ansel Adams, Isadora Duncan, and photographer Cedric Wright. Jaime de Angulo, a leading expert on the vanishing languages of American Indians, lived just above Jackie and Wallen. As he hired and soon fired de Angulo from Berkeley academia, famed anthropologist Alfred Kroeber objected to the "erratic and unstable behavior of de Angulo, a man known to have indulged his passions with both men and women (at times dressed in women's clothing)."[14]

Florence Boynton, another unique neighbor, taught boys and girls to dance in her Temple of the Wings up the street. According to neighborhood lore, the term *Nut Hill* originated with the lunches Mrs. Boynton packed for children to take to school. Much to the amusement of their peers, the lunches consisted entirely of nuts and raisins, which the Boynton children of course tried to swap for the bologna or American cheese sandwiches most of the other kids ate. Everyone knew the Boyntons danced wearing togas in a family home that looked more like the ruin of a Greek temple than a normal house. So it was the kids at Hillside School that named the neighborhood Nut Hill, capturing the Boyntons' cuisine and the hillside's lifestyle. Historian Charles Wollenburg nods at this explanation in his own account of the term's origins: "The residents . . . were engaged in social and cultural experiments, involving new concepts of living spaces and lifestyles. . . . The name may have referred either to the vegetarian diet of some of the residents or to the fact that some hill-dwellers had lifestyles their fellow citizens considered downright weird."[15]

People such as the Boyntons were drawn to the Berkeley hills in those early years of the twentieth century. The rolling green hills, oak trees, and redwoods were inviting; and Berkeley, because of the university, was becoming "a city of scholars, a crossroads of cultures and a magnet for visionaries. This unique combination of ingredients provided fertile ground for individuality, eccentricity and creative expression."[16] Bernard Maybeck was the perfect archetype of this new, distinctly American spirit. And something interesting was always going on in Berkeley. Sheila's daughter, Katherine Sorensen, remembers that in Berkeley of the 1950s there were rumors of tumultuous discoveries being made by Robert Oppenheimer and others at the Lawrence Berkeley Laboratory, in the hills above 2751. "Of course, Jackie invited the scientists from the lab to her home for dinners and parties."[17]

Even today, Lloyd and I live among some wonderful characters with fascinating histories and robust opinions.

FALL

JACKIE AS EM

At the end of the Second World War, Wallen was transferred to Germany. Jackie thought this would be an exciting opportunity for the family, as the twins had just graduated from high school. They joined him in Frankfurt, where Jackie recorded the experience in a book-length story she titled "Journey: Small Adventure."[1] She writes in the third person, assigning her own thoughts and emotions to Em, the heroine of the story. This work is a departure from the writing she had done in her diaries; later, she would use the same device of a thinly disguised narrator in stories in which her cat tells the story. In "Journey," names are sometimes changed and sometimes not; Wallen, for instance, is the Major, but the twins retain their real names. The story was never published, and Jackie made only two copies, one for each twin.

Through the character of Em, Jackie writes perceptively about an awakening American woman living in Allied-occupied Germany, a country with a rich and dreadful history. It is also the story of how this time abroad changed Jackie and her family.

It begins in September 1946, as Em, Cherry, and Sheila travel across the United States by train:

> *Rain and cornfields and pumpkins and red barns, God, what a wonderful country America is! Em loves the Wyoming cow country—its clean desolation is like her thoughts—thoughts that go back aching to the loves and the sureties that are left behind. Em feels she will never again be able to fashion for herself a life like that of the last two years, a life like a crystal cup, dangerous to hold but clear and brimming full.*

Is Jackie referring to an existence unencumbered by in-laws and a husband? When she says "sureties," does she mean her mother and the ranch? I recall Jackie's writing about the pleasures of her Hilltop garden where, "left to [her] own devices," she would "sit with my back to the warm stone of the house and just look and dream."[2] Until her "small adventure" in Europe, Jackie seemed to take uncommon enjoyment in such simple pastimes. In her diary at the ranch, written just before the trip, she said, "I am lost in dreams, un-fathomable, un-sharable, lost in the pieces of myself that the sun has melted loose and that I shall gradually make into a pattern."[3] Her thoughts were turning to her future, as she began to think seriously, not just dream, about what kind of creative work she desired for her life, going forward. The exhilarating freedom she enjoyed in Germany would help her find the answer.

Em had daydreams, too. On the train to Chicago, she "woke out of her coma" and got the two girls, six suitcases, and packages onto another train, all in thirty minutes. She meets a woman in transit who looks forward to army life in

Europe, "free of a flock of parasitic relatives for the first time in her over-burdened life." Em hears that familiar story again and again among the other traveling wives. In New York, Em and the twins stay in barracks, waiting for their ship. There are "Negro" wives and babies there, and the southern wives "screamed loudly that they would not eat and sleep in the same rooms with niggers." The army shrugs and says, "Go home if you prefer."

Em has an unorthodox idea about these traveling wives: "What a terrific expense is incurred by this insistence on one particular woman for one man. In come hundreds of British brides, out go thousands of American wives. The Eskimo simply borrows his friend's wife when away from home and think what millions it saves."

On September 7, 1946, Em and the twins sail the Atlantic on the *Zebulon B. Vance*:

> *The days go strangely and quietly; the hours move from meal to meal, bedtime to deck time. To finally see land of a morning, the cold and rainy coast of North Germany, to stand and shiver on the deck and wonder what was ahead . . . and then to see the picture postcard country with desperate ruins. The excitement picked Em up and carried her through meetings and greetings and down the shabby busy dark streets to the cleanest little house in the world.*

In Hoechst, a district of Frankfurt, Em meets her landlady-to-be. Frau Hanni had farmed out her three little boys to make room for Em and the twins, but she remains in charge of the house. Em sits and sulks, thinking how she likes cleaning her own house, working her own garden, and organizing it all: "Now I am willy-nilly a member of the leisure class and feel like a parasite." Later, she realizes that it takes a squad of workers to run a German household, and Frau Hanni begins to count on Em for "aid and succor in any domestic crisis."

Parties and gatherings begin; the beautiful seventeen-year-old twins are invited to dinners and for rides on motorboats down the Rhine. One day, while visiting the Major, General Eisenhower walks by, "slim and smiling, a fine face to see." The family takes excursions to Wiesbaden, Munich, and Stuttgart, visiting castles and cathedrals in their indispensable Jeep. "Feelings go up and down with the thermometer and the days' activities." Em and the twins study German with Herr K., who is "almost tearfully grateful for coffee and a cigarette," and they take classes at the local craft school, trading lessons for a chocolate bar.

"October leaves are yellow and the woods are sweet and cool, primitive, ageless, elfin woods." Em wonders if travel can keep one eternally young, for now she feels as she had in New Mexico and New Jersey: "There too, she had made a new home, become a new person—she was so busy learning new customs that the old self seemed lost. Em had shed matronly, smug habits and was forced to become young and sharp and alert again."

The radio announces the hangings of Goering and von Ribbentrop, and Em is momentarily pulled back to wartime Germany and the dark mood of the people. The constant cold and lack of heat are a difficult change from life in California. Em hates the cold. Wrapped in her cozy feather quilt, she

> *contemplates a new and perhaps snowy world. She woke up feeling like an oyster, surrounded and warm and*

Jacomena and Wallen, 1947.

Photograph courtesy of Maybeck family.

Left to right: Sheila and Cherry Maybeck, n.d.

Photograph courtesy of Maybeck family.

secure. She became tangled in a web of German words. I am now inarticulate in two languages, she thought. If I were a German I would spend most of my time in bed.

Living in Germany made it easy for Em to visit nearby Holland where her parents were born and raised. Em's first trip to Holland is a dream, "a challenge of the fairies. Once a little girl in California sat under a madrone tree and listened to her mother's stories of a land of beds in closets, tea in the morning, of clean forests and heather, of tiles in the hallway, and canals and coziness." Em and the twins fall in love with Amsterdam, staying nearby with cousins, sleeping under a thatched roof. Together, they visit Haarlem, where Em's grandfather lived above his store. Uncle Karel looks a lot like Em's father and is full of welcome and questions. Em loves the windmills and the crooked, narrow streets full of bikes and handcarts. She discovers how the Dutch coped after the war:

It's cold but life moves strongly, urgently, hopefully. The ration for the people was one egg in six months but they did without to get dollar credit to buy back tools lost in the war. It seemed miraculous after the desolation of Frankfurt to see windows full of clothes and fur and silver and leather, even shoes, but they are rationed. Dutch people eat about every two hours and it takes a healthy constitution to keep up with them.

Home again, Germany again, utterly cold and gray, you feel as if the cold had walked down on her big tired feet. And we were folded again into a world of Army wives at the beauty shop with no hot water and no liquid shampoo. A snug, warm world of selfishness.

Left to right: Sheila, Marianna, and Cherry, Holland, 1947.

Photograph courtesy of Maybeck family.

Van Huizen store and home in Haarlem, Holland, 1947.

Drawing by Sheila Maybeck.

In December 1946, Em travels to Paris with a friend, Natia. They sleep on newspapers in the train, settling down for the night on the "dark green cushions with their dark green smell." The beautiful Parisian stores are full of perfume and lingerie, and they dine on an "exquisite lunch near Rue Rivoli—potato soup, a creamed fish patty with a black mushroom on top, and a baked apple with meringue."

> *Em had decided to have a wonderful day—to find a man, a rather wonderful one, and not be alone in Paris. In the bus she looked them all over and decided and smiled and there he was. A tall young Dane to stand beside in Notre Dame, have lunch with. It is an enchantment, a quick comradeship based on that intangible bond between people that makes a friendship.*
>
> *Em glowed and sparkled in her fur coat and gleamed wickedly when she met Natia after lunch and had to admit that she had acquired a young man and could he come along too?*

Jacomena, n.d.

Photograph courtesy of Maybeck family.

It is easy to imagine handsome Em charming the men, confident of her attractiveness. Did she share her adventures with the Major? Up to this point in Em's story, it seems to me to be autobiographical of Jackie's experience in postwar Europe, perhaps with a few imaginative flourishes. Outside of Em's tale, Jackie left only a bare-bones account of what went on during this important year in her family's life. On the other hand, what better way to capture the magic of being in a new and strange place: you can become someone else entirely.

In Paris, Em and Natia navigate the warm subway and tour castles and dark forests. Yet "I am homesick," says Em, "for the green grass on the hills at the ranch and red Toyon berries for Christmas in California." Back in Frankfurt, the travelers are met by the "efficient twins, beautiful stacks of mail, and two inches of snow all over the world. Em says 'Nuts to travel,' and climbs into bed."

Several times, Em visits an art school in Offenbach, where she experiments with local porcelain clays and glazes. She now realizes that she wants to work with pottery when she gets home: "Em will become an artist!"

Among the parallels between Em's travels and Jackie's actual life, Em's flirtation with being an artist is particularly beguiling. Sometimes Em seems to be like an imaginary friend, a stand-in, with the freedom to go places her creator can't. But something undeniably powerful is getting stirred up here.

Em's Christmas is cold and spare, with few joys. Frau Hanni had saved three skimpy candles for a wreath. But "Em would love to kick up a little violence, a little activity. She could feel

Hoechst, Germany, 1947.
Drawing by Jacomena Maybeck.

tiny changes in herself of adaptation toward this life and this place." By New Year's Eve, Em writes, "bells are ringing, a new sense of starting afresh and of things about to happen."

In the chapter "Dim January," Em takes a bus to meet the Major, surprising herself with unfamiliar impulses and actions. "So many people got on, that Em got all giddy and gone, and thrust herself out like a cannonball, and absolutely amazed all the soldiers trying to fight their way in."

January brought an elegant cocktail party, though Em had to get herself there in a snow flurry. She was asked to be especially nice to a Dutch Commander who didn't take much interest in Em. She decided she just wouldn't try and when Em won't try she raised a high black wall around her with no loopholes. So up went the wall and there was Em trying to peer around it, just in time to

> *see another woman be perfectly charming to the Commander and carry him off to see her etchings.*
>
> *"Well" said Em, pushing her wall over and coming out before it was too late, and the Colonel from West Point, the psychologist, and the Greek Diplomat were snapped up. She went into action fast and became very attractive and redeemed herself in the eyes of her hostess.*

"White February—the cold goes on and all the human cave-dwellers pop out, and look about." Em and the twins again travel to Paris; but this time, Em gets the "golly-wobbles." After a day or two, she knows their cause: she does not like the noise and hustle of cities, "and the hot mob, in spite of the handsome bartender and his twenty-year-old tawny port, in spite of the endive and tomato salad, the martinis in the little bar, and the lacy underwear." She leaves the twins in Paris, happy to return to the bitter cold of ruined Frankfurt. "Apple cider, and not champagne for me; bread and cheese rather than tarts; that is the kind of human I am so let's get on with it." She is not reconciled to the German weather, though:

> *March should be Wild and Strong; a bit of sun is good for the soul and the bones, but everything seeps and slushes and runs. Even the sparrows are wet and soggy looking. Em is in an arguing mood: "Mr. March," she said, "we do it better at home. There are acacias and daffodils and small pink plum trees in bloom. Not disgusting frozen cabbage and earth exhausted from the winter's pressures."*

Em has had enough; she wants to go home, and she knows just where that is. She has not been sleeping well for a month, and visits the army doctor:

"You seem to have a simple anxiety complex. Go and see a psychiatrist." Oh, thought Em, laughing and crying inside, just let me get home to my house and my garden and the Berkeley sun and fog and the work I can do there and I will be all right. Just help me out 'till I get there.

As if on cue, new orders come out the next day. "Orders that are always around the corner in the army, waiting to change your life." They must leave Frankfurt for home on March 19, Em's birthday. Suddenly, "it is raining, it is thawing, the sun is breaking through—a rebirth after the death of winter. Em has a song in her heart—going home, going home, we are going home, home where my heart is!"

And then came the shock, the not too unforeseen event to catch the breath and the heart. One twin wants to stay and get married to a Fighter Pilot with curly hair and blue eyes. She was eighteen on March tenth and is serene and sure. Em woke at five and walked the floor and wept and searched her soul.

The twin who wants to marry came down with her Captain and she was beautiful and serene and let her parents argue around her until they were exhausted and all their arguments fell flat and they began to say, "Well, if we do let you get married, perhaps you could have the silver and the sheets and the dishes. It is no use our taking them home and you buying new ones." So the twin smiled and everyone became quite excited and happy.

That night, Em slept fitfully in the great cold room. She woke and did not know where she was but struggled out on the balcony and found the night sky and the garden smells a reassurance. This was the day, Em's birthday and her daughter's wedding day!

John Bathurst appears in Em's story in the same role he played in real life—as the groom. He comes for Jackie and company at ten in the morning and the party heads to the Burgermeister's office for the stiff German civil ceremony required by international law. At four, everyone drives to the beautiful old village church where the Episcopal service is a "little pageant that fitted in completely." Sheila and John walk out under crossed bayonets. And there is the young captain, "perhaps still wondering, 'How did this happen to me? I am the bachelor type.'"

Sheila and John Bathurst's wedding, 1947.

Photograph courtesy of Maybeck family.

That night, Em, the Major, and Cherry take the train to Bremerhaven—"a jail, full of unhappy people waiting for ships." What a long and extraordinary day this has been for Em—an ending and a beginning. She would not miss Germany, she would soon be home again with the Major and Cherry, but she would dearly miss Sheila.

Em writes in detail about the long trip home, as people begin to cope with the return to their civilian lives:

> *But her insomnia persists—the nights are like a secret life that she leads while the Major and the twin are fast asleep.*
>
> *Storms, seasickness, the lounge full of men smoking cigars, few chairs. Ship rises twenty feet on the rollers and comes down with a shuddering bang and her propeller spins out of the water and the men in the cabin below say they sleep mostly on the ceiling as they are tossed up. Em would lay on a bench on the deck with her head on the Major's lap while a Sergeant and a WAAC made love in the corridor.*
>
> *Everyone is miserable and bored with each other but still being humorous and beautifully, humanly patient. Moods are changing. The world is coming at them again. The temporary friendships of the sea are dissolving. People no longer have the strong need of each other.*
>
> *Em prowls the decks and found Hugo beside her on the deck. They stood and laughed in the darkness and the wind, and laughing and wet, they kissed each other. Hugo's kiss was as strong and concentrated as his card playing, a wild pleasure in the moving air. He said, "I will remember that even the worst voyage can have a beautiful memory" and he let go of Em and she fled.*

Desire suddenly ignites as if out of nowhere; and just as suddenly, it subsides.

Now it is March 1947, and Em can see a little gray line on the horizon—America! Passengers stand on deck all day and watch it grow closer. In the rush of these last parts of Em's story, Jackie speaks from her own heart as she anticipates the end of her adventure:

> *And now the circle closes. The dear familiar faces of friends are closing it, the few important unique people who are the color and the savor of life. The last seven months are as a yeast within me, was a thought that moved deep within Em.*
>
> *I can feel ideas thrashing about. They will become a gift to my friends and a part of my thought pattern—bigger, more liberal patterns for my having been stretched around this circle and made to see and feel and do new things.*

The Jacomena who returned from her real-life adventure was a changed woman. A more mature self had emerged, based on a new blend of elements from her early life. There is a stronger and more conscious identification with the Dutch people, whom she had found steadfast and industrious even amidst the postwar devastation. She had gotten glimpses in Frankfurt of herself as an artist and writer—a vision that would carry her into the future.

Jacomena, 1946.

Photograph courtesy of Maybeck family.

Although the senior Maybecks had once again occupied High House, they moved back to the Cottage just as Jackie and Wallen arrived home. That simplified homecoming. Life on the Hill resumed without Sheila; Cherry lived at home and went to UC Berkeley; Wallen rode the ferry to the phone company; cousin Thea's daughter, Teddy, came to live with them; and Kerna and her husband were now in their home at 2780 Buena Vista Way. Possibly for the first time since she had moved into her new home fourteen years ago, Jackie felt she could take full possession of it.

After her adventures in Germany, Jackie's desire for creative work blossomed into a plan: "Pottery and clay were the only things that satisfied me at all."[4] She was so impressed with the work they were doing at the California College of Arts and Crafts in Oakland—fellow students would include Manuel Neri, Nathan Oliveira, and Peter Voulkos—that she enrolled full-time. Now, at age forty-six, Jackie had arrived at a turning point in her life—a chance to develop something of her own.

> *I began to call myself Jacomena when nobody was looking. My mother called me Jac with a Dutch accent and Flo always called us JacandWallen. So when I made pottery, I began to sign them Jacomena—there were many Jacks!*[5]

Jacomena completed her master's degree at the California College of Arts and Crafts in 1952 and acquired a reputation for her beautiful glazes, especially the celadon tones. She once remarked to my husband, "You can learn the whole history of civilization in the study of glazes." She would work with clay for the rest of her life.

Jacomena, n.d.
Photograph courtesy of Maybeck family.

FREEDOM AND LOSS

The 1950s brought more changes to Jackie—not so much of place (as had been the case in the 1940s) as in her family. In June 1950, she carried a tiered wedding cake to the ranch to celebrate her parents' fiftieth wedding anniversary. They had emigrated to California in their twenties and made a home for their family out a long country road, miles from town. But in July, Helene had a slight heart attack and was worse by the end of August. She spent her last weeks in Berkeley, dying at age eighty-two. Jackie wrote, "She smiled and was pleased and looked happy—and was gone."[1] Sheila remembers Jackie being similarly composed about the loss; "She didn't let us know her feelings; it was all very quietly done."[2]

Jackie's father, Pieter, returned to the ranch alone. "He rose at sun-up and walked all over the ranch—little trails, smoking his pipe, and relishing the sight of early deer, birds, squirrels—and how the grass grew, and winter water made new little streams."[3] He lived there by himself for several more years, walking the twelve miles into town three days a week. A notice in the *Ukiah News* announced his tragic death in 1953: "[Pieter Renzius van Huizen III] was burning

Jacomena, Helene and Pieter, and the twins, 1939.
Photograph courtesy of Maybeck family.

brush near his home and fell. While unconscious, he suffered burns which caused his death."[4]

Fascinated by the central role the ranch played in Jackie's and the twins' lives, I asked Cherry whether her mother had visited it after Pieter's death. She said she had not, but that in the early 1980s, Jackie's cousin Amelius had come from Holland on a "memory trip." He went through Ukiah, out Low Gap Road, and traveled half the length of Pine Ridge Road before being forced to turn around by the roughness of the road. Cherry's vivid description of the route intrigued me:

It took an hour to drive the 10-mile ribbon of writhing, life-supporting road connecting Ukiah with Pine Ridge. It wound through hot hills of smooth tan grass sprinkled with Live Oak trees; it forded summer dry creeks filled with Dogwood and cool lichen-covered rocks. It went past the Signet's shack, alive with dirty kids and trash, past the schoolhouse with its nostalgic smells of chalk, lunches and books; past the "Buggy Shed" and down the long curving sunny south grade to the well-tended orchard of the Koturba's farm where the gates began . . . to be opened and closed again for passage over the neighbors' land.

Following the creek, the road narrowed; banks high and unyielding on one side against which car fenders rubbed as drivers carefully negotiated the curves, astutely avoiding the precipitous drop to the busy creek on the other side. . . . Only the familiar or very courageous would have found their way this far. There was no turning back.[5]

Like cousin Amelius, I wanted to see this land. Would the house still be standing? It would be over one hundred years old. What made this place so "real" for Jackie, and could I feel this too? In early 2019, my friend, Susan Kanaan, and I explored the area around the ranch. Imagining ourselves in Maybeck's elegant Packard, we headed west from Ukiah (where Susan lives) on Low Gap Road. Veering onto Pine Ridge Road, we slowly navigated the deep potholes of the narrow county road, remembering Jackie's stories of traveling in mud and rain. The landscape became more verdant, with boundless meadows and mature oaks blanketed in lichen and moss. We followed Orr's Creek and then entered the Robinson Creek watershed, which used to supply salmon to homesteaders. As my city car rounded Devil's Elbow, feral horses galloped straight toward us, then disappeared, leaving us breathless.

Neighbors in trucks stopped to inch past us and ask our business. We picked up Susan's friend, Gina Campbell, who has lived on Pine Ridge Road with her husband since the 1970s. She told us these passing encounters on the road are mostly where the locals see each other. Gina guided us to neighbors who live even farther out Pine Ridge Road. Noni and Jerry Chaney's place is an oasis with a pond, gardens, waterfalls, and panoramic views of Pine Ridge itself. The couple has worked for years to carve this paradise out of wild fields and boulders. While we savored her wild-berry cobbler, Noni told us that her grandparents, Annie and Anthony Dory, bought their land in 1913, the same year the van Huizens bought their first one hundred acres. To my surprise, Noni flipped the pages of her scrapbook to a deed for a piece of property sold to her father, Albert, in 1941 by Annie Maybeck. On an old map, the Maybecks' land appears right next to her parents' plot. When I held up Sheila's drawing of the van Huizen house, Noni and Jerry said, in chorus, "That's Mory's house! It's still there."[6]

Noni led the way up a hill and pointed to the largest tree in view, one ancient redwood that now wholly conceals the old van Huizen house. As a young child, she watched Jackie's father climb the ridge in his tall black boots and big coat, en route to town for supplies; he'd stop by Noni's house to visit on the way back. She treasures two van Huizen wagon wheels leaning against her chicken coop.

I was thrilled to be right there, so close to the ranch Jackie adored. I could understand how she longed for this countryside with its endless vistas, sweet smells of clover, and sunshine. Now I was eager to explore the old van Huizen property. But I would have to wait awhile longer for permission to pass through private gates to the ranch.

Perhaps because I was so close to the old place where so much had transpired, thoughts about Jackie's history crowded in my head. She never wrote about her feelings of losing her father nor did she mention the circumstances of his death. His loss left her with the question of what to do with the land.

> *We kept the ranch just as it was for a year, it was peaceful and dreamlike. The loveliest place I'll ever know. How I loved it and my people there, who were so good to me always!*[7]

Selling it must have been a difficult decision; so much had happened there. But "her people" were now gone. And it no longer felt like home.

Jackie loved the feeling of the sun on her back at the ranch, and looked for another place to spend the often-chilly Berkeley summers. Margorie, her friend from army days in Alamogordo, had moved to Taos, New Mexico, and urged Jackie and Wallen to visit. In the 1950s, Taos was a lively and diverse art colony; Georgia O'Keeffe, Ansel Adams, and D. H. Lawrence were drawn to its rich culture and beautiful landscape with the fourteenth-century Taos Pueblo at its center. Jackie bought a house for $1,000 out of her grocery money and went ahead of Wallen, whitewashing the walls and oiling the floors to get ready for the season:

> *Everybody was so light-hearted and light-footed and coming and going, you know. . . . We were broke, and so we invited each other for dinner, and it might be just a big stew. . . . The fine art of gossip! . . . People were swapping husbands and wives and all kinds of weird things.*[8]

Back in Berkeley in the fall, Jackie and Wallen tackled big projects on the weekends. Jackie was still in her master's program, and needed a potter's wheel and kiln so she could work at home. Together they hand-built a studio behind 2751 out of cement blocks, calling it the Pot Shop. Soon it was overflowing with Jackie's work.

Jackie had long dreamed of living in a level house. I have wondered whether she contemplated trading houses with Ben and Annie, who were then in the Cottage. At that time, the Cottage had only one story, with a warren of rooms and a level yard perfect for gardening. But perhaps the Cottage was just right for the senior Maybecks, now in their old age. They gave Wallen and Jackie title to a lot up the hill from 2751: "This was too steep to stand on: the bad lots were kept for the family. We knew how to handle them."[9] Ben Maybeck, then in his eighties, started planning a level house with Jackie and Wallen's ideas in mind. It would be his last design.

At some point, Jackie decided that Ben's enormous beams were not right for the house, and argued with Ben, "Well, I have to live here, I'm paying for it, Wallen and I, and we can't go on with these beams."[10] They were re-milled as Jackie requested. The couple worked every weekend, pouring the enormous fireplace themselves, two feet at a time. Neighbor Robin Pennell has a vivid memory of Jackie pushing a heavy wheelbarrow full of cement: "She was tall and somewhat thin but she was so unusually strong."[11] They called the house Arillaga after a name printed in gold on a secondhand door recruited for the entrance.

Jackie writes, "We always thought we would live there, but then when it came right down to leaving this house [High House] . . . I had a Pot Shop here by that time, and Wallen had his basement workshop."[12] Each time Jackie and Wallen built a house—and there would be one more after Arillaga—it added to their responsibilities; but it also helped shape the simple and rustic aesthetics of the hillside community.

At about this time, daughter Sheila and her husband, John, back from Europe, were living in Oxnard, in Southern California. Jackie's first grandchild, Adrienne Bathurst, named after her Aunt Cherry (Adriana), was born in 1953, adding a fourth generation to the Family.

Now, in the early 1950s, Ben and Annie would walk the path from the Cottage to 2751 to see what Jackie was cooking. If it looked good, they would stay for dinner. In the photo on page 138, the Maybecks are sitting in the Cottage's cozy winter living room with windows facing the Bay. The graceful willow chair in the foreground was made by a craftsman who would drop by every spring to repair it (in the winter, bugs ate its legs off) or sell them another version.

In 1954, Jackie planned Cherry's wedding to Wade Nittler, "inch by inch, from the cake and the dresses to the guests . . . and everything."[13] Cherry had become a physical therapist, having been partially inspired in that career by none other than Ben Maybeck, who used to rub her back

Arillaga, #2 Maybeck Twin Drive, Berkeley, California, n.d.

Illustration by Bernard Maybeck, courtesy of Maybeck family.

Left to right: John, Annie, Adrienne, Ben, Sheila, Jacomena, and Cherry, 1953.

Photograph courtesy of Maybeck family.

Ben and Annie in the Cottage, n.d.

Photograph courtesy of Kathy Brown.

and tell her how important it was to keep one's body in good shape.

With Annie and Ben now in their eighties and early nineties, respectively, Jackie decided to fix up the Cottage; and this time, she took charge of the project herself. She added an open pergola of railroad ties which stretched from the back door to the new garage, creating an outdoor studio for Ben. "I am absolutely insane about levels instead of stairs, so I planned it so that the kitchen floor and the pergola and the garage are all on the same level."[14]

Changes kept coming. Jackie had lost both her parents at the beginning of the decade, and now, midway through it, Annie Maybeck had a sudden heart attack and died at age eighty-nine, with Ben at her side. Jackie spoke frankly about her complicated relationship with her mother-in-law:

> *[Annie] was a lot of fun as long as she was not pushing you into a corner. She had a very sharp tongue. She would say "you've got lipstick on, take that dirty lipstick off your face!" She'd say that, just like that.*
>
> *So I was always on my guard with Little Grannie, but I admired her a lot. When she was dying, I went to the hospital and she said, "Oh, Jackie, thank God you're here." Then she faded away and died.*
>
> *I drove away from the hospital and I felt uplifted. I suddenly felt that now I can be friends with Little Grannie. I had a very strong feeling—I can't explain it—but it was the recognition as though she had been freed of something. Maybe she'd busted loose from her little tight, puritanical knot. Now I could be friends with her because she had changed, not me.*

Jackie felt that she, too, had been set free. She deeply valued the Dutch self-reliance and independence that had allowed her parents to carve a ranch out of the wilderness; but this highly developed sense of independence and confidence often put her at odds with Little Grannie. At the same time, Jackie deeply loved the Family. Perhaps she dealt with this ambivalence by becoming the sort of person who dances close and then moves away, beyond reach.

After Annie died, Ben, then ninety-three, moved from the Cottage into High House with Jackie and Wallen. Jackie writes that Kerna, whose idea it was, never so much as asked her about it. Jackie was teaching glazes at the California College of Arts and Crafts and running a crowded household that now included Sheila and her three-year-old daughter, Adrienne, while John was stationed in Iceland. At first, the arrangement with Ben seemed to work. As Jackie put it:

> *In a way it was hard on me and in a way it wasn't . . . [Ben] was a very sweet man. . . . He always wanted to be in on all the things that people were doing. He loved to sit at the table and have people come and have coffee with him.*[15]
>
> *He came to all the parties and was the center of the stage. He told all the ladies that they were beautiful and would be more so as they grew older.*[16]
>
> *But Ben was demanding and if he wanted two dozen pink pearl erasers the fire flared up and everything stopped until he had twenty-four pink pearl erasers.*[17]

Sheila tells a favorite story from those days:

> *One day, Ben was drawing and told me he needed a charcoal drawing pencil and I said, "We'll get it after*

lunch." Then he pounded the table and said, "I need it right now—I might be dead after lunch." Three-year-old Ade marched up and told him, "Don't you talk to my mother like that." He stopped pounding on the table and after that, lunch was a success.[18]

Ben Maybeck at 2751 Buena Vista Way, 1956.

Photograph courtesy of Maybeck family.

After living with Ben for more than a year, Jackie went off on her own to visit friends in Sag Harbor, New York. Before she came back, she told Wallen that she wasn't coming home if Ben was going to be in the house. "I'd got to the end of my endurance . . . I always felt that Kerna should have taken him part of the time."[19] So Wallen moved Ben, who was largely bedridden by then, back to the Cottage in late summer with his nurse, Inez. Jackie returned; and two weeks later, Ben died in the middle of the night on October 3, 1957, at age ninety-five.

One can imagine Jackie's feelings of grief, as she had endured a long decade of losses. Her parents had died, the ranch was sold, and now the Family was gone. The era of "everybody depending on each other, seeing each other all the time, carrying around each other's packages"[20] was over. Perhaps, though, the transition also brought her a sense of relief and readiness for the future, along with an end to her worries about the old folks.

It was time for a new era. Wallen retired from the phone company, and he and Jackie finally had their home to themselves. Jackie's reputation as a fine arts ceramicist grew as she exhibited her work at the Pacific Coast Ceramic Exhibitions, the Association of San Francisco Potters, and the California State Fair, winning numerous prizes.

And by 1960, Jackie had six grandchildren to enjoy.

Just after Ben died, a flurry of activity erupted on the hill. Kerna and her husband moved from their home at 2780 Buena Vista Way to the Maybeck Studio and built a house on the corner of La Loma and Buena Vista Way. The William and Kerna Maybeck Gannon House was completed in 1959, but shortly afterward, the couple moved to Southern California. Despite her recent differences with Kerna, Jackie would miss her.

Perhaps inspired by Kerna—or just because they loved a project—Jackie and Wallen again resolved to build a level house. They sold a lot near 2751 to finance a paved loop road. The road supplanted an old dirt trail, dubbed Via Tito in honor of a donkey that had belonged to Kerna and Wallen as kids. The new road was christened Maybeck Twin Drive after Cherry and Sheila. For the first time, Jackie and Wallen

Left to right: Jacomena, Wallen, and Kerna; Wallen's retirement party, 1958.

Photograph courtesy of Maybeck family.

Jacomena's grandchildren, Santa Cruz, California, 1962.

Photograph courtesy of Maybeck family.

Jacomena and Wallen at 2751 Buena Vista Way, 1961.

Photograph by Ted Streshinsky, courtesy of the
Berkeley Architectural Heritage Association, Berkeley, California.

Jacomena's ceramics.

Photographs by Pam Valois.

Jacomena's small ceramic animals, circa 1980.

Photographs by Pam Valois.

drew up their own plans for a house. It would be built at the top of the new Drive. Jackie planned the fireplace with a hob to put her feet on, just as she enjoyed at 2751, and cut the decorative railing with an electric jigsaw. They set the ceiling beams on fire to bring out the grain. Completed in 1960, it was called Buckeye House, after the handsome neighborhood trees planted by Ben Maybeck. To no one's surprise, "We didn't live there, but we went there and sat by the fire, sometimes."[21]

Jackie and Wallen wanted a sunny place to take the grandchildren on weekend trips, and developed yet another project. They bought a small house next to a river with swimming holes, in Cloverdale, eighty miles north of San Francisco:

> *We'd all go up in the cars and open the car doors and everybody would fall out and start doing something they wanted to do. . . . One summer we all made paintings. . . . We built and rebuilt . . . we rebuilt the bathroom; we rebuilt the kitchen. We were busy all the time. Then we'd go to Arthur's to have a drink and dinner, walk across the creek up to our waists in water.*[22]

WINTER

JUST JACKIE

It was there, right in the midst of their Cloverdale weekends, that Wallen suddenly died in July 1962. Cherry vividly remembers, "He had a heart attack at the house and I tried to resuscitate him. He'd complained about being tired after one of our rafting days. Jac and I took him to the hospital in the middle of the night. When the kids woke up, he was gone."[1]

Wallen was just sixty-four years old. He had grown up in the Berkeley hills, roaming dirt paths on his donkey, Tito. His life was filled with family, pageants, hiking, books, hunting, and a career at the telephone company. He'd married the love of his life, and fathered twins. As is natural, he may have expected to live as long as his parents had.

Now just sixty-one, Jackie was truly alone. She told me how she felt about this when we talked in 1980:

> *I was bowed down with responsibilities and cares without anyone to discuss it with—without asking for help. Before, I had felt utterly irresponsible and frivolous—things would always come out all right. There was Wallen, the Family, and the land to count on.*

Wallen Maybeck, 1954.

Photograph courtesy of Maybeck family.

She thought about changing houses again, and could have her pick of the several houses she owned. But perhaps with the recent peaceful years with Wallen, she was now comfortable and content with High House. She moved her bed into the twins' room where the sun streamed down through the fanlight window above. Her grandson, Scott, remembers that she would tie a scarf over her eyes to keep it dark, as Little Grannie had done with the twins at naptime.

Jackie continued teaching at Arts and Crafts but came home to an empty house. A friend suggested she invite Yukako Okudaira, an adventuresome nineteen-year-old Japanese woman, to live with her. I talked with Yukako, now an artist living in New York. She was surprised that Jackie did not talk more about Wallen at the time; she "kept her sadness to herself."[2] Jackie wrote to Sheila, "I'm so glad I have my Japanese girl—she is someone young and alive in the house—she is sweet and strong and does everything to make me comfortable and I have to figure my time coming and going around her, to help her get places, but it's worth it."[3] The affection was mutual:

> *Jackie was so kind to me, taking me everywhere and introducing me to friends. She'd put on her work gloves, her hat, and her bikini and clear the brush from the islands dividing the two roads of Maybeck Twin Drive. No older woman in Japan was like that!*[4]

Jackie turned to her daughters for support. Cherry lived nearby in Santa Cruz, and Sheila and her family were in Japan, where her husband, Johnny, was stationed. Sheila saved Jackie's letters from that time, and her daughter, Katherine, generously shared them with me. They are personal and candid, revealing Jackie's moods as she coped with widowhood. Filling thin sheets of yellow paper with her large, flowing cursive, she wrote, "Yuka says I must be feeling cheerful—I was humming today and didn't realize I had not been."[5] Jackie had been to Davis that day, visiting Kerna, and felt cheered up. She put on old clothes and helped move furniture into the new one-room unit she and her cousin, Red Kleyn-Schoorel, had created from the Cottage garage, anticipating her first tenant, Victor Seeger, an instructor of physics.

A year after Wallen's death, Jackie shared reflective and optimistic thoughts as she considered visiting Sheila and John in Okinawa:

> *And at long last, I can get away from here for a spell and look at myself and who and what I am now. Without Wallen I am different—I must find my own directions, where before I could follow his—ours—pool our ideas and come up with what we wanted. I don't like just living for me. I feel I should take myself out and polish me up and see what can be done with this article, this me in which I sit.*[6]

Jackie left High House in the care of Yukako and a professor who was renting rooms, and flew to Japan for a long two-month stay "of love and nearness."[7]

> *And there I was in Berkeley with no one I belonged to. I blindly put things in order and went to Okinawa too, in the spring of 1963.*
>
> *I found it wonderful! The smells . . . the beaches . . . and water like liquid jewels. It was so hot I couldn't*

Jacomena in Okinawa, Japan, 1963.
Photograph courtesy of Maybeck family.

sleep. I couldn't bear it and put on my grey kimono that made me invisible and I slept in a deck chair behind the house.

Of course I couldn't just stay there. I had a house to care for in Berkeley. I sadly tore myself away. I loved Okinawa; it was the most interesting place I ever visited.[8]

Back in California, having let High House until September, Jackie bunked with friends, Fran and Peg, for the duration, but drove home to chop weeds along the Drive. I laughed when I read that she'd had to hire a truck to haul the weeds, because this seemed as incongruous as a farmer giving away her crops. Jackie had always harvested brush to stoke the great fires she built in her huge fireplace, hoping to drive out the chilly Berkeley air.

Jackie's letters to Sheila reveal a growing sense that this period wasn't just an experience of absence or total loss. There are signs that she began feeling alive again, and that sometimes this life was enough.

> *Oh—and do save some letters—I so wish I had my mother's and Wallen's now! It's hot and I have all the windows open—I love having everything open—I should live in a tree!*[9]

She drove to Cherry's Santa Cruz home, where they read Sheila's letters from Japan to each other. The three of them loved to sew, sharing patterns and coveting the Japanese cloth Sheila sent to make skirts and suits.

Jackie started discovering how to be happy again. "I haven't really found me yet—it will take awhile, that sense of happiness in being—just being—that comes sometimes. I went out today and did a naughty thing. I bought a leopard cloth sport coat—fun! Here's a drawing: that's me for fall."[10] Her life picked up momentum:

> *I'll teach one night a week at [the Arts and Crafts] school. Then dinner at the Women's Faculty Club with Peg, or tickets to the Shakespeare play at the Greek Theater—it was a lovely warm evening with all the Berkeley people climbing up there in the half dark—reminded me of college days!*
>
> *The maple and sumac are a lovely autumn red and I always sort of celebrate autumn—I even change my clothes and perfume. But the little maple is so lovely—I hang over the balcony and look.*[11]

By the 1960s, there were ten houses on Maybeck Twin Drive, and Jackie owned and managed several of them—"which was a delight but also time consuming." Mr. Fisher, her renter in the Cottage, sent a card "to a wonderful Lady of the Land," making her think about her new role:

And that's really what I want to be—not a landlady. It's too much for me, both in work and money. Really it's the work—jobs I thought nothing of with Wallen but I just can't tackle alone. How I worried last night when it rained hard but it stopped by morning and all is well. I walked up to Buckeye house at nine in the morning and put in another post, making a sort of plank fence below the stone wall as a water drain.

Taos is sold and I keep being grateful that it's no longer mine to worry over and keep up. I drive along being relieved![12]

Jacomena in Taos, New Mexico, circa 1963.

Photograph courtesy of Maybeck family.

I was confused about which houses Jackie still cared for and managed in the sixties. In a letter to Sheila, Jackie explained that "Ben and Annie left the land to Wallen, not to Wallen and me, so I have to pay a great deal for it. Damn, but I'm lucky anyway, no use being greedy!"[13] She went on to say that Sheila and Cherry would own the Cottage, the Cubby, and half of Arillaga; and she would own 2751, Buckeye, two lots, and the other half of Arillaga. Hilltop had been sold, and it is unclear who owned the Studio. Jackie was thinking about Wallen as she wrote:

> *I'm doing some tall thinking. Wallen would want me to do something good with all this and I feel he'll help me find it. He wouldn't leave me miserable if he could help it, so he couldn't help it and I shall gradually stop being miserable. And do something fun and good and include him in it.*[14]

Jackie took care of the houses and of herself. The tenants could, of course, be a handful, and Jackie (although typically a generous and flexible landlady) maintained a few rules of her own about the properties—she had lines which were not to be crossed. Victor Seeger, who lived in the small unit (the former garage built at the front of the Cottage) when we were there in 1977, lived there for a total of twenty-five years. "The rent was very low and Jackie never raised it all those years."[15] He now rents the Maybeck's Arillaga house next to us, and remembers the time a fellow renting the Cottage criticized Jackie's cousin, Red Kleyn-Schoorel, saying he worked too slowly. The next day, Jackie invited the tenant to leave.

In a rambling but carefully crafted letter to Sheila, Jackie wrote that she looked forward to having a new roommate—her old friend Ivy Jean—after Yukako's departure, though she added, "I was alone for so long that by golly, I got used to it and began to like it!" She continued:

So that's the news of the hill. I should run but I want it to be a good letter, not just a scrawl. Isabele took us to dinner at the Anchor. Ruth brought Sewell, higher than a kite with two drinks and four women, and he played the piano, loved everyone! Glad Donn and Robin didn't see us! Ruth and the "men at the Corner" came to dinner last night. I had baked beans (deluxe) and salad and flan . . . and a fire. They aren't thrilling but certainly nice.

Maybe I'll go explore the mother lode country—I crave the trees. I sure miss those endless rambles Wallen and I took. Anyway, restless old Jackie is all ready to roll again![16]

But there was always more than enough to do, some of which Jackie wasn't keen about; but she needed to stay busy.

I had lots of jobs. There were the houses and I had my pottery. Pretty soon your work begins to engage more of your attention and it creeps into the spaces that were occupied first by your mate.

You begin to find yourself. You change your format and your attitude towards things. Being a widow gives you tremendous freedom, suddenly, more than you can handle at times. I think of freedom now as something you have to work for very hard.

She told me that you must recognize that your freedom exists. Then,

> *You must renovate your head—go into your mind and see what you've got to work with. Do you have lovable features, do you like to work, do you like to hide? Who am I and what do I have to work with?*

Jackie felt "free in a scary sort of way. First in a vibrato sort of way. I can handle it and I'll get married again. Then it just didn't happen." She didn't want to replace Wallen, but she felt like "half a person." She told me years later that at age sixty-one, she'd thought of herself as "old as the hills. If I'd known more about age then, as I do now, I might have started a very different life. I felt that finally I was growing up and I didn't like it very well." I wish I had asked Jackie what "different life" she might have created.

Good news came from Sheila and Johnny. They hoped to move back to Berkeley and the Cottage from Japan when John retired from the Air Force in 1964. Jackie was thrilled:

> *You can do anything to the Cottage within reason—certainly you may choose a good stove and double sink. Whee! You can glass in the lanai and make an outdoor patio in back. We could have folding doors into the kitchen—think that one over—cut trees, etc. etc. But I don't want to do anything until you see it.*
>
> *Oh my—oh my, I really get all of a twitter! I bought three flame-colored hibiscus for a hedge for you in front of the garbage can. They should remind you of Okinawa!*[17]

Jackie also wrote an encouraging letter (she called it a "Sermon") to Johnny, who had just had another bout of pneumonia:

> *I wouldn't bother if I didn't love you. I believe you are still operating on your war training of heroism and stamina. It's not 1941 any longer and your life now is based on quite different principles. We don't need your physical effort and prowess; we need your brain, your ability to think and figure out—to get along with people—to tell stories and make us laugh.*
>
> *So take care of that body which you push so hard! The body should be relaxed and rested, the mind alert and ready for anything. Love, Jackie.*[18]

At last, in summer 1964, Sheila and John arrived with their three children in tow. The Cottage bulged with kids, cats, and dogs; little John-John, age four, slept in the bath-tub. With help from the senior John, Red Kleyn-Schoorel designed and built an upstairs bedroom with windows to the trees; Jackie excavated the hill behind the downstairs bedroom, enlarging it with a wall of cinder blocks; and they eventually enclosed the pergola with a roof and windows on both sides, calling it the Summer Living Room. The Donn Pennells, across the Drive, had five children ready to play with the newcomers. Jackie wrote, "It was busy at the Cottage, not easy for Sheila, but I loved to have Sheila and Johnny close."[19]

Since her wedding in 1947, Sheila had followed John, living in army housing, dreaming of having a home of her own. In a recent conversation with Sheila, I was not surprised by her mixed feelings about those days, which were reminiscent of Jackie's own feelings on the subject.

It was kind of an empty time—we were back in the Cottage but I never truly felt that it was my house. I did things on it but it was hard. John was there for a while, but then he went up to Seattle. Jackie was ok, but she wasn't being overly happy to have us there. She was always good, humorous, attentive, but not squishy-loving. Maybe it was just the Dutch way.[20]

Sheila had hoped her girls would walk to Hillside, the neighborhood school; but in the 1960s in Berkeley, students were bussed to school across town. As Adrienne and Katherine rode a bus home, a girl burned Adrienne's arm with a cigarette, "so the kids took the bus straight to the police station! Can you imagine?"[21]

Despite such challenges, Katherine, then age seven, remembers the magic of those years in the Cottage:

In the mornings, I would just run across the street, open the rickety gate, climb up the path past the mulberry tree and open the big wooden door with the huge Chinese gong . . . even at the entry, there is a suggestion of a fairy tale world here. I was looking for the big wicker basket I knew to be full of toys. And Mug root beer was always at my beck and call. I could always find Jackie sitting at the head of her large dining room table, a bright blue placemat positioned neatly in front of her. She'd have her cat, Amanda, on her lap and a cup of tea close by. Jackie was usually writing.

Jackie is a stunning woman—her eyes are what strike you first—brilliant blue and clear as the sky. She can light up the world, she can embrace you with those eyes. You know the moment she looks at you that you will never be judged. She is the biggest influence on my life.[22]

Katherine and Adrienne visited Lloyd and me recently at High House, opening a flow of memories for them. As small children, they had looked forward to weekends, when they would jump into bed with Jackie to have morning tea. We walked across the road to visit our friend, Kathy Brown, who now owns the Cottage. Katherine insisted that it was she who slept in the bathtub, and not her brother, John-John, as Jackie had declared in her memoir. And as she climbed the Cottage stairs, Adrienne recalled their dad burnishing the new railing with a torch, as Ben Maybeck had done. The little wooden desk was still in the living room. They remembered the coffee nook with the blue plates, and the parquet floor in the summer living room that buckled in the rainy season.

The Cottage, now with a glassed-in lanai, 1965.

Drawing by Sheila Bathurst.

In 1969, Sheila and her family unexpectedly moved to Seattle, where John had been offered a job in an insurance company. This left Jackie alone again, to manage Buckeye, Arillaga, the Cubby, the Studio, High House, and the two Cottage units. Of these houses, she said, "They are like children, always a problem, a leak in the roof, a sewer stopped up."[23]

And again, for both better and worse, there were the renters. Jackie had enjoyed Yukako's company and continued to offer rooms in her home to students. She wrote to Kerna, "I could use a Soul Mate. Meanwhile I make do with students around to give the illusion of family, and dates with Al and John for a different companionability—a gentle love."[24] When we talked in 1980, Jackie had just scolded her current boarder, Peter:

> *I always come upstairs in the morning to make my tea, feed the cats, water the garden, and then I go back downstairs and have my tea and talk on the phone with Flo to see if the sun's come up at her house. Then I come back upstairs again and here is Peter—he is sitting in my chair eating his breakfast with his papers spread all about.*
>
> *Finally last week I said, "Peter, why do you always sit in my chair? All my life in this house, that has been my chair, and I want it free to sit in when I want it." I said, "Make yourself your own spot—find a comfortable place." He's kept out of it ever since.*

In the 1970s, Anabel Cole, a postdoctoral student in plant and insect virology at UC Berkeley, occupied Jackie's south bedroom for the grand sum of seventy-five dollars a month, including food. Annie became another of Jackie's

Jacomena at 2751 Buena Vista Way, n.d.

Photograph courtesy of Maybeck family.

tenants whose lives were forever changed for knowing her. She and her fiancé, Gray, were married in the great room of 2751 in July of 1981—the only wedding there to that point. Annie admired Jackie's daily schedule:

> *She'd wake up to tea and her Pillsbury croissant, play with her cats, and then head outdoors for physical work. She kept the islands clear of brush and the trees trimmed away from the road. Of course, she could tar a roof and level a stair. After lunch came careful accounting of her rental houses. She lived simply and could make a chair or fashion a dress to set off her collection of Navajo jewelry.*[25]

In one of Jackie's fanciful cat stories, Alvin and Albert, two principals in a dynasty of cats, gossiped about the state of the Cottage across the street: "For eight years bushes grew wild, the plumbing stopped up, plums rained down and made a mess."[26] Jackie, her granddaughter Adrienne Bathurst, and four cats moved into the Cottage for the summer and spruced it up. Jackie "cleaned, painted, and polished and scrubbed. She put in an upstairs bathroom. Floors were tiled and painted. Windows and doors stood open and sun flooded in."[27] By 1977, the Cottage was ready for a new set of fortunate tenants.

Jacomena and Alvin, circa 1977.

Photograph courtesy of Maybeck family.

SAVORING THE GIFTS OF AGE

The grace with which Jackie greeted her final season is one of the treasures I most value from knowing her. She continued to record her introspective, emotional life through letters, diaries, and journals. Through these, I am better able to understand the choices she made to free herself from the burdens of the past, without fear of the future, keeping herself level. Her life in this season was peopled with friends of differing ages and backgrounds; and she ruled easily and happily as the matriarch of the Maybeck clan. The Maybecks had helped her create her own unique blend of simple and very imaginative taste. Perhaps having lived her life so closely intertwined with the life of a great architect had helped her realize that becoming an artist was part of the answer to the question posed to her as a young woman, "What did I want to be?"[1] Jackie transformed the experience of growing up a ranch girl into an identity as a woman that included running electric cement mixers and cutting brush to keep warm. She relished roadwork and holding a grandchild at least as much as throwing a pot or writing a story.

When I met Jackie in 1977, she was more than twice my age. She had left teaching and simplified her life by selling two principal properties, the Cubby House and the Studio. She prized her friends and family, and kept them close to her heart and to High House. Moving out of the deep shadow of prematurely losing Wallen had made her more flexible and adaptable. Finally, after years of taking care of others, that profound experience of loss nourished her gift as an artist:

> *These years since Wallen died—these years are like a tree that began to put out little leaves and blossoms where before, it was a bare tree. It began to grow. It was sort of abundant, it took a while.*
>
> *The creative person has to create something for himself to do, something that's not a fast pleasure. I don't think you can stop being creative. You might say you're tired out and can't do anything else and the first thing you know, you're digging in the garden or you wander by the Pot Shop and you start fiddling with the clay.*
>
> *Wherever I go, part of my mind is looking, looking, and sifting through ideas—it's there always, always.*

For Jackie, a privilege of old age was that she could now make things just for herself—she no longer felt obligated to compete and make things that would look good in an exhibition. "These days, I calibrate the work against the pleasure. When you're doing it for yourself, you make the greatest picture or pot." She continued to miss Wallen's support. "I had lost my strong right hand and therefore I became afraid of doing big projects like another house or big pots. If I were a real genius person, I'd just ignore that and steam ahead by myself."

After Wallen's death, Jackie never built another house, but she continued to remodel and add to the several she owned. More and more, she was comfortable making decisions on her own.

> *Sitting with a cup of coffee by the fire I think out problems and plan improvements. There is a special panel in my head for worry things. Let them stew awhile and a solution pops up.*[2]
>
> *Walking through the Cottage today, I thought that just starting a house would never give you all the cute corners that we get from adding something every few years.*[3]

Cherry explained that Jackie didn't enroll High House, or her other houses, on Berkeley's registry of landmarked houses because she wanted to be free to make changes as she wished. It was a Maybeck tradition to improve houses and remodel them to fit the occupants' current needs. Jackie had helped build or renovate six homes in the neighborhood of Nut Hill—the Studio, the Cottage, the Cubby House, Arillaga, Buckeye, and High House—as well as Hilltop, summer homes in Taos and Cloverdale, and, of course, the ranch.

Jackie told me that she liked change, reminding me that every ten years she and Wallen had done something different. "Not that I'd ever sell this house [High House]!" Now, as she approached the age of eighty, she was comfortable owning High House by herself, and planned to live there forever. At the time, Lloyd and I so strongly identified Jackie with High House that it was not until I discovered the history of the house and her evolving attitudes toward it that I began to understand she'd at times felt this magnificent house wasn't her own. Thinking about her future, she quietly said to me,

> *For me, living here is a bit like living on the ranch. This is the heart of the family—anyone who needs it can come live here—I can always live here with help.*

As Lloyd and I stood in the front yard of the Cottage in 1977 and gazed up at the striking lady on the roof for the first time, there was a sense that our timing was perfect. Jackie climbed down, juggling her tar pot, and we tried to have a casual conversation with her about renting the house, hoping she wouldn't guess how very much we wanted it. Like old Mr. Maybeck scouting a new client, Jackie proposed she come to our San Francisco flat for lunch.

Whatever happened (and as previously mentioned, our parrot claims the success was entirely due to his romancing Jackie), it worked, and we packed up to move in. Jackie rented the Cottage to us for $400 a month. Our thrift shop sofas and odd collection of painted wicker chairs filled the two living rooms. Pepe—unused to life in the Rousseauian paradise in which he now found himself—had a hard time on moving day, shouting "Help! Help!" as Alvin, Jackie's real-life cat, passed under his perch in the apple tree. Our dining room was the little nook that jutted out into the garden—we lingered over coffee, imagining Bernard Maybeck in his claret beret enjoying his doughnuts. A sliding door divided the winter living room and nook from the kitchen and summer living room. On a cold morning, we'd rush to cook breakfast in the drafty kitchen, looking forward to getting back into the cozy nook. We bought thick red velvet curtains at the Salvation Army to lock in heat from the wood-burning stove. Our king bed fit nicely in the white cement block bedroom with its view to the Bay. Lloyd took the upstairs room for his office, and I converted a downstairs room into a darkroom, carrying water from the bathroom. We planted our first flower garden and dreamed up more ambitious plans, only to be confronted by an unexpectedly steely response from our normally easygoing landlady. We were not allowed to enlarge the flower beds—nothing was to compromise her lawn!

Our years in the Cottage were halcyon years for us. I worked part-time as a dental hygienist and studied photography, and Lloyd started his practice as a psychologist at Kaiser Permanente. Others who have lived in spaces designed by Maybeck have remarked on the way his houses became important partners in their lives. It was certainly true for us. After nearly a decade of dating, breaking up, and passionate reunions, it seemed we had found a missing piece in the puzzle of how to live, with Jackie at its core. I was attracted to her joie de vivre, her enthusiasm for a new blossom in the garden, and the way she could design a beautiful pot. With Jackie's and Lloyd's encouragement, my photography found a focus, as she truly embodied the "gifts of age." Jackie encouraged us to get married, never mentioning her own past ambivalence about that institution.

Once we decided to get married, we could think of no better place to exchange vows than in our own front yard. We packed annuals into the flower beds, gathered food, and hoped for sunshine. We were glad Jackie had defended the lawn; it made a good place for our family and friends, including Jackie and Flo, to gather. Music filled the summer living room as friends played the harpsicord and flute, and

Left to right: Pam, Jacomena, Lloyd Linford, and Pepe, 1979.

Photograph by Pam Valois.

Winter living room of the Cottage, 1977.

Photograph by Pam Valois.

Summer living room of the Cottage, 1977.

Photograph by Pam Valois.

Jacomena at the wedding of Valois and Linford, July 1978.
Photograph by Pam Valois.

an Episcopalian priest who was also a Jungian analyst read the vows we had written.

As we spent more time together, Jackie and I discovered that we enjoyed sharing projects. She loved to write and I loved to take photos, so together we cooked up some articles for the *Berkeley Independent and Gazette*. My favorite one was about the seasons in Berkeley:

> *The spring starts with the pink plums from Japan. . . . Just before the plums come the Chinese magnolias—a frame of branches and nothing but exquisite single flowers. In March my little Eastern maple is all over rosy packages. End of March green stems come out from which hang the seeds, the little red wings called keys. . . . In March also the wisteria comes to town. . . . Crane your neck a little—the eucalyptus trees are in bloom. . . .*

There's no use going into berries and autumn. This would become a book.[4]

From the fruit of the plum trees behind the Cottage, Jackie made tasty preserves, and she baked tea cakes from the persimmons on the trees along the Drive. We shared suppers on our patio, sometimes including Flo. Across the street, Jackie created celadon-glazed bowls and teapots at her potter's wheel, and hand-fashioned whimsical little animals at her sunny living room table. We and our friends coveted them—they always sold first at her Chimney Potters' group sales, so we learned to go early to get something signed "Jacomena." Over the years, we acquired a set of celadon bowls but hid them away while our boys were young, afraid we would break them.

For Jackie, taking care of the Hill was still a big responsibility. She explained to me:

My chore is the Hill. I feel that I am the last of the Maybecks and I feel obligated to take care of it as long as I'm here. I see that it stays clean, the dead trees get removed, that the road doesn't grow over with grass and weeds, the road is repaired, and the people fit together, to keep a sort of neighborly feeling going.

As long as I'm here, I can protect the land. I think possibly Cherry and Sheila will help; they feel the same way. But unless you live here, it doesn't work. Pam—you come and project yourself.

I was pleased and surprised in replaying this interview to remember that Jackie had suggested I move back to the Hill and "project" myself! At the time, in 1980, I never imagined having the chance. Her charge is something I think about in my current role on Maybeck Twin Drive, having returned in 2013.

Jackie set a tone in the neighborhood, way back then, and we are especially grateful for the way it has endured. As new houses went up on the Drive, Jackie encouraged people's capacity to create and work together. She recalled the day she was relaxing in the sun with Kerna and suddenly heard a chain saw starting up. Walking up the Drive, she saw three of Donn Pennell's trees down, and quickly summoned neighbors who showed up with hatchets, saws, and sandwiches.

Jackie and Wallen helped establish what would become the Maybeck Twin Drive Association, which continues to provide a framework for working together as a neighborhood. Maybeck Twin Drive is still a privately owned street, and association members gather regularly to discuss emergency access and how best to maintain the narrow road and the brush-covered islands that divide it. The meetings have given Lloyd and me the unexpected experience of having neighbors who have become good friends and fellow travelers. There is a congenial spirit—a desire to know each other and each other's families. Jackie blessed the neighborhood with her magic. She, and the Family, modeled an unpretentious lifestyle that was worthy of the houses. Her spirit of fun, generosity, and creativity still touches all of us. Without her, this would be just one more street in Berkeley.

Our lives in the Cottage continued in 1977 and beyond. We would swap tales with Jackie about the various characters on the Drive and exchange views on politics. One day when she was craving sunshine, she and I splurged on an overnight trip to California's Gold Country. She stripped down to her bathing suit, not at all self-conscious of her

Pam and Jacomena, Jamestown, California, 1979.
Photograph by Pam Valois.

long, wrinkled limbs, and we spent the day swimming at the National Hotel.

As Jackie and I grew closer, I began to worry about losing her. I wanted to capture something of her spirit in a portrait—in Susan Sontag's phrase, "to symbolically possess her."[5] Jackie agreed to sit for a photo, and many more versions followed from that first sitting. Intrigued with the subject of aging, I began interviewing and photographing other older women in hopes of creating a collective portrait of the challenges and potential riches of aging. As I listened to their stories, I learned that in old age, many women felt they had been released from the burdens of the past and were now free to act independently for the first time.

Seeking subjects for this project, I arranged to photograph M. F. K. Fisher, the legendary author of *How to Cook*

Jacomena in her Pot Shop, 1980.

Photograph by Pam Valois.

a Wolf, a classic on food and culture. Mrs. Fisher agreed to meet, and requested that I bring along Jacomena Maybeck, of whom she'd heard. One of my favorite stories of that time took place on the day when Jackie, Lloyd, and I drove north to Mrs. Fisher's ranch in the Valley of the Moon for lunch. MFK, who had just turned seventy-two, saw eye to eye with Jackie on their philosophies of aging: "Well, good girl, Jacomena, you've really fought for this time of life. One needs to have been alive mentally, lived fully and with thought. It's ridiculous to wait until you're sixty-five to develop yourself—how dare anyone do that?"[6] With that out of the way, MFK announced she'd like a drink before lunch, and Jackie immediately agreed to join her. Lloyd was appointed to make martinis, and instructed to mix them "ten to one." A novice bartender, my husband wasn't sure whether "ten" referred to the gin or the vermouth; but conscious of the age of his clients, he opted for ten parts vermouth. Fortunately, he sampled this mix before serving it and immediately realized his mistake, slyly adding a load of gin. The lazy afternoon drifted by; I photographed MFK; and the two old ladies drank us under the table.

In 1980, Charlotte Painter (my coauthor of *Gifts of Age*) and I asked Jackie if aging brought with it any special benefits for a woman. She replied:

> *You remind me of one of the privileges of being older. You can have an awful lot of fun with younger men because they are no longer afraid of you and afraid you'll snatch them into marriage. So, I have about five young men about fiftyish that I'm very good friends with. I'm not having affairs with them! Men can relax with an older woman and enjoy themselves—this makes a very nice*

kind of friendship. I go out with one man to the opera, and on botany walks with another.

While my girl who rents the north room is on vacation, I've had her boyfriend, Peter, to myself for two weeks. He marches up the hill at five thirty—we have a small dinner and maybe a glass of wine and then we sit around and watch the news and talk a bit. Gradually we've become so comfortable. I suddenly realize that I'm enjoying Peter very much. But then along back comes his girl and snatches him away and that's all right because I'm not making any attachments.

Although the roster of Jackie's family members changed over the years, with losses and new additions, the love and support she received from her daughters, Cherry and Sheila, were a constant. "They shone like little stars in our lives," Jackie wrote.[7] Cherry summed it up for all of us:

She's the kind of person who makes you feel better about yourself for having been with her. You can make a big mistake, but she never says, "I told you so,"—just, "how can we handle this?" And it's never repeated back to you again. Mother has few negative feelings, and those she has are directed against rudeness, smallness, bad manners, ungraciousness and selfishness. She can be icy, brisk and determined if confronted by these! She is ageless, and there is no generation gap in her presence.[8]

As time went by for us in the Cottage, Lloyd and I began to feel a growing desire to own a home and start a family. With Jackie, we dreamed up a plan to build a tiny house in the "secret garden" behind the Cottage lawn, but realized that it wouldn't really fit. We were all thinking about what to do.

I was pregnant in January of 1979 when Jackie wrote an essay, "The Small House." It reminded Lloyd and me that a tiny house for two was quite different from a house for a family. We'd have to leave the Hill.

> *Let's talk about small houses. . . . If I, myself, today, in a world of skyscrapers, wanted to build a little house I would and I could. It's so simple—a box with one side tilted to shed rain. I think in simple plans and simple materials. But I also know how to swing a hammer and an axe. . . .*
>
> *There is a need and there is an answer. Two rooms imply two people or more. . . . The single person in a town or city rents a room and that is his hidden world of rest and restoration. This person marries and at once feels the need for more space. He now needs a house—four—six rooms. It can still be simple. . . .*
>
> *The first necessity after the primary retreat is a place for friends, for social life. The house is stretching with family and is filled with the toys man accumulates for the enrichment of his life, no matter what size his house.*
>
> *The End*
> *Maybeck*
> *January 1979*[9]

We resisted moving and leaving Jackie, but life moved on. The feline storytellers, Alvin and Albert, lamented, "And then came the beautiful couple. They had their wedding in the garden. . . . The cottage glowed and sparkled. Then they bought a house of their own and left. We all cried."[10]

In 1979, Lloyd and I bought our first home—a six-room bungalow in North Oakland, adjacent to Berkeley. It was a rough transition for us, starting over on a busy street with houses packed in next to each other and no view of the sky. But Zack was born in this house; and soon we received a note in the mailbox written on a stiff slice of yellow poster board:

There is nothing like a Baby—
The most snuggly and cuddly
They don't go out of style
They always are beguiling
Even if not smiling.
It's the nicest thing to do—
Having a baby by you.
Love, Jackie

We kept in close touch with Jackie, having her to dinner or joining her and Flo at High House. Together we planned Annie Cole's wedding in July 1981, and filled 2751 with flowers. On another day, in a different house clinging to a different hill, Jackie visited us and we complained about our lack of a sidewalk. She sent a note afterward, including her detailed October 1982 weather log written on an envelope:

Thanks for the coffee on the patio and berry soup. This was my month of October last year. We only had one hard rain—28 Oct. If you ever want me to help pour a piece of sidewalk with you–I could bring tools and bucket etc., not hard to do—a few good hours. You all looked so good! Love, Jackie

Jacomena and Scott Linford, 1988.
Photograph by Pam Valois.

When our son, Scott, was born, she wrote, "What a love of a baby! Two sons—are you proud?"

Our boys enjoyed visits to Jackie's house. We'd have tea with toast and, of course, homemade plum jam. Scott remembers the edible orange flowers on the path to her door, and Zack loved playing with the cats. One of my favorite photos is of Jackie and Scott in our yard, working on an art project.

In our absence, the Cottage did not sit empty for long. Soon it was full of college boys and Cherry's sons, Scott and Mark Nittler. The cats, Albert and Alvin, gaily noted, "Cars come and go, boys shout, study lamps are on all night, Clyde the dog romps, Fat Cat sits on the roof. Like old times. The cottage is all alive and well."[11]

Later on, Jackie's grandson, Scott Nittler, and his wife, Susi, lived in the Cottage for a year. "We'd go over to Jackie's for supper—a chicken leg and a potato—and come home and make another dinner. But I've never forgotten

The Cottage, 1983.

Drawing by Jacomena Maybeck, courtesy of Maybeck family.

the experience of living there, or the love and admiration we felt for the lady who presided over it, Jacomena."[12] As the Maybeck family still owns Arillaga on the Drive, Scott manages it and patiently presides over the Maybeck Twin Drive Association as our elected president.

When we visited Jackie in the 1980s, she talked of nothing but her latest project. Feeling prosperous, she had helped her granddaughter and her husband, Adrienne and Dan McGuire, buy a 1920s craftsman bungalow in Santa Cruz, near Cherry and Wade. With Jackie's deep experience and usual enthusiasm, they modernized it "inch by inch."[13] Jackie loved the house and, according to Dan, chose the best room for herself—"and she deserved it. It has the most windows, and she designed the French doors to the garden because light was so important to her."[14] Outside, she shoveled dirt into ditches that had been created by storms, hoping to level the ground. Adrienne recalled, "Jackie worked like crazy! She liked painting but would only use a brush, saying that a roller would not do a good job."[15] Later, Jackie frequently drove the winding road to Santa Cruz in her big green Plymouth to help with her great-grandchildren. "She came down and made food, did dishes, held babies, fed them, read stories, and introduced them to art when they were older. What a blessing she was!"[16]

In her eighties, Jackie became a well-known historian. Friends and neighbors celebrated the debut in 1980 of her book *Maybeck: The Family View*, an intimate account of the Family that also includes notes about her own life. She proudly talked to me about new interests and the benefits they brought her:

> *I've gone into so many things I didn't do before—like writing the book with Flo or my book about Ben. We were asked to give a talk—and suddenly I felt a great satisfaction in feeling that somehow I'd acquired a point of view and usefulness that I'd never had before.*
>
> *By rolling into it, you begin to find out what you have in your own head and do something about it. That's what the books were. A lot of relationships developed, and that's been so satisfying. You become a personality instead of just being a person.*

Jackie was now the spokesperson for all things Maybeck, leading tours of her houses and giving interviews to writers and architects hoping to hear original stories about the Family. Many assumed that she was Ben's daughter, as Kerna had moved away by then. Jackie's popularity grew and she became a bit of a legend, just as she had predicted back in college. Her lifestyle and her wit—not to speak of her amazing memory for the family history of which she had been such a key part—made her the perfect guide.

In a lovely introduction to *Maybeck: The Family View*, Alan Temko, architectural critic for the *San Francisco Chronicle*, wrote:

> *Of all these Maybecks, each paddling a separate canoe on the high seas of independent family life, Jacomena seemed to me the most strangely lovely. In a sense, as a Dutch girl coming from Java, she was literally a stranger, but so was almost everyone else in Berkeley when she arrived. Rather, it was in the freedom of her presence, unanchored, but so perfectly attached, not only to Wallen, but to the intangible Maybeck quality which she helped to shape as much as any of them except Annie.*
>
> *Her devotion to Ben, the soft, glancing attention that had in it the understanding of a true spiritual daughter, herself an artist, was part of the overall mood, as much as the quick warmth of sunlight when the fog straggled out of the eucalyptus.*[17]

Temko's description of Jackie as Ben's spiritual daughter is fitting. She, more than anyone, carried on the Maybeck name and style after the others had gone.

In addition to a long and rich relationship with the patriarch of the Maybeck clan, Jackie shared Ben's experience of being raised by immigrant European parents.[18] She watched his genius for creating with simple materials, and adapted that as a key part of her own artistic style.

Jacomena and Ben Maybeck at the Palace of Fine Arts, San Francisco, California, 1950.

Photograph courtesy of Maybeck family.

When *Gifts of Age* was published in 1985, Jackie helped host a celebratory party. This was fitting, because I felt that Jackie truly understood my work. She appreciated that the women in the book were selected because of their current ways of life and outlook and their capacity for meeting ongoing challenges with vitality and optimism, not because of their past accomplishments. A favorite quote from the book is from Julia Child, who said, "A passionate interest in what you do is the secret of enjoying life, perhaps the secret of long life, whether it is helping old people or children, or making cheese, or growing earthworms."[19] At the book party, the women I had photographed shared their impressions of sitting for a formal photo in their old age. They had never seen themselves so close-up, wrinkles and all, in a photograph; the camera freezes a single expression in a way we never see ourselves, since we're usually in motion.

To this day, I am struck by how often Jackie's name comes up in conversation on the Hill. It's almost as though she were still here. Evelyn and Jon Rantzman lived next door to her for ten years, beginning in 1986. Jon, who reminded me that Jackie's famous plum jam always included the pits, also had other vivid memories of her:

> *Both of our houses were falling towards the street, so here's Jackie in a bikini pounding little wooden shims between the bricks to prop the house up. She was definitely a fan of deferred maintenance, and, of course, liked to solve things herself. She'd prune the ivy in her bikini, making little piles in the garden, and then, without waiting for it to cure or dry out, light a fire with it—the smoke was terrible.*
>
> *Jackie was a great neighbor. When her good friend, Ruth Pennell, became senile and asked to go see her husband, Jackie would take her home, saying "Ruth, he's been dead for twenty years!" Jackie was straight off the shoulder, no b.s.*[20]

Jon suggested that the reason the neighborhood was called Nut Hill was not just because four Nobel laureates, the Boyntons, and several famous professors (such as Charles Seeger, the pioneer of American musicology) lived here; "It was also because all these octogenarian women were running around being healthy and assertive people."[21]

Siegfried Brockmann, who has owned the Studio for many years, recalls that among other guests, Jackie's dinners always included cats. "The cats had full range—they were up and down on the dinner table like regular guests. The Dutch tolerated different things—you can do what you like whenever you want—everything is okay until it wasn't. Then Jac would not bend on it."[22]

I chuckled in recognition when I talked with Roger Raiche, who had first rented in 1988 and later owned the Cottage:

> *The thought of moving to the Cottage was very exciting, as Jackie had said I could garden around the house. But from the very beginning she insisted that the lawn remain. She was fine with all the clearing and replanting, but was obsessed that I didn't remove any of the lawn. Anytime I cut a few inches into the "lawn" to expand a bed, she had a fit. She told me she was going to send her daughters over to measure the square footage of the lawn, so if it was less when I left, I'd have to restore that portion.*[23]

Living in our High House today, I better understand the variety of tasks that confronted Jackie. The gardens are large and sprawling, with several different levels. Weeds and rodents proliferate between houses, winter leaves cover the walkways, and ambitious deer discover holes in the fragile fencing. The old wooden railings are rotting and often need replacing. I remember Jackie asking me,

> *Did you see my new railing down in front? I felt I needed it because my friends were getting so wobbly. I took two years stewing about it but I was lazy and didn't want to tackle it alone. I guess I could afford to have a man come in and add pipes. But then I thought, I have a four-by-four redwood post and I have a good post-hole digger and I know how to soak it in creosote. Then a young man came along who needed extra work and I thought, My railing!*

I said, "Let's go up in the black acacia woods—I know where there is a tall sapling about sixteen feet long." We needed another little tree so we went up the hill to our forest and a neighbor had just been trimming his trees and we noticed a branch at the bottom of the pile. That night, we sneaked it out and carried it home and oiled the branches with linseed oil. The railing looks just right, as though it's always been there.

When you interview Flo tomorrow, she'll say "Old age? Ridiculous!" She's home today with a chest cold. It's an interesting life, isn't it? What about a cup of tea?

Jackie kept up a lively correspondence with daughter Sheila, then in Seattle, elucidating what was on her mind in her eighties. Perhaps she wrote letters, rather than making phone calls, to continue the art and craft of writing, working to keep them interesting. She continued her daily log of the weather and events, but no private diaries of that time have been found.

Dearest, dearests!
I had much brush to cut at the Cottage. Now home and Rudi cat is on my lap—tapping my chin—hopeful for a handout. Now I must check my priorities and get some work done:

#1—1st dump Rudi who is drooling on me.
#2—Decorate 3 little plates so they can dry.
#3—Be here for the man who wants to buy some Maybeck drawings.
#4—Make applesauce to can—I got a bag of them in Sebastopol.
#5—Go say hi to Tanny who is just back from her trip East.

#6—Try to remember the other things—maybe buy some pansy plants?
#9—Go see Bernadette's kiln at 2 p.m. Mail this letter.

Love to you all—have some crispy-frosty days. Love, Jackie.[24]

Dearest Sheila,
I went out into warm early sunshine and pulled some weeds with the lovely sun on my back. I was working on repair of the wall behind the kitchen and removed a vicious geranium—he made bad smells which finally got to me.

I was going to go into skirts on May 1st but it's too cold here. I do love my prairie skirt.[25]

Dear Sheila,
Here I am in my favorite cafe in one of those comfortable, padded orange booths. If it's not crowded, I feel I can write as well as eat. This morning, the boys at the Cottage were out sawing and splitting wood—such a good ranch sound![26]

Dearest Sheila,
I'm still all happy from talking to you—I've turned on the furnace and am sitting up in bed. Outside it's gray sky and wind blowing trees—ugh to that. But my cinerarias are a symphony of blue and purple and rose!

It's the restless mood—the restless wind can hit anyone, anywhere. Even on the ranch—which I loved so much—I do remember thinking "oh if only something would happen—anything!" So now that I have my day arranged, I feel good again and energy pours in. Guess I'll make some cookies for Fillmore.[27]

Dearest Sheila and all,
I have seven small pieces and some tests. I also have started making ducks—in a sort of spring rage. I can always fill up the living room with ducks to dry! Am trying to figure how to cut my wild lawn—so wet—maybe a scissor.[28]

In her late eighties, Jackie was still corresponding with her first tenant at High House, Yukako Okudaira:

Dearest Yuka,
Sitting at my table in warm sun, but the city is lost in fog. So—I bring in wood for the fire, drive to market and buy vegetables for dinner—we eat with the seasons. I go up and down the scale of being absent-minded and burning the dinner, to giving a good tour of the house.
All good wishes for your best New Year ever, Jackie.[29]

Now in her nineties, Jackie called Anthony Bruce, director of the Berkeley Architectural Heritage Association

(BAHA), to say it was time for them to do a tour of the houses on the original Maybeck property. The BAHA events committee agreed, calling the tour "At Home with Jacomena Maybeck and Her Neighbors" and suggesting that each house serve a snack or have music for the guests. Knowing that some houses would serve fruit and nuts, Anthony badgered Jackie to come up with something interesting and "Maybeck-like."

Finally, Jackie decided on donuts and coffee, insisting that, "Ben [Maybeck] really did love to sit in the nook at the Cottage with his donuts and coffee." Guests enjoyed Odile Levant on the accordion at 2751 [High House] and a zither player at the Studio, while savoring Mrs. Barneveld's ginger cream and butter cookies. The tour was a success. At the end of the tour I looked over at Jackie sitting on the couch, all in red—she looked radiant, like a queen.[30]

We celebrated Jackie's ninetieth birthday together. Our boys had known her their entire lives—they knew her as an artist living a unique life up on the Hill, and as a very special, very old woman. They made her a chocolate cake with lots of frosting. We hoped she would live forever.

Jackie must have guessed that she would live a very long life. When we talked in 1980, she mused:

I guess I'll feel old age creeping up on me when I get to my nineties. Our whole society is geared on that—we calibrate old age with deficiency, with lack of energy, lack of good looks, with an inability to get around freely, and that to me is the package we call old age. I'm not ordering any of that. It probably means being in a wheelbarrow!

Zack and Scott Linford with Jacomena, 1991.
Photograph by Pam Valois.

Now it occurs to me that people go through so many phases—Ben was always physically easygoing and became reconciled to sitting in the sun and dreaming in his nineties. That's the way old people in the cottages in England used to do—they'd sit by the fire.

When you get to the point where you have no energy, then, for goodness sake, make yourself be placid and accepting. Sit in the sun with your hands folded. Don't complain. That's a privilege too—a lot of people in the world never have that time.

This acceptance of aging—understanding and savoring the gifts of each decade—touched all of us who knew Jackie. Her wisdom grew as she aged, and she was rewarded in this last season of her life with a good mind and devoted family and friends.

At age ninety-one, Jackie wrote her memoir, *People & Places: A Memoir*, in the lyrical style I admired in her letters and Christmas cards. I love her wry advice for continuing to garden in spite of limitations imposed by age:

> *And there is what I call Grandmother Gardening. . . . A Grandmother Garden should have a couch and a comfortable chair to view the garden from. . . . The deer and I have compromised: they get the lower garden to sleep in, to eat everything, maybe to have babies in the bushes. . . . A grandmother can weed and plant any flowerbed as wide as her arm is long. Long-handled pointed hoes are great! Toy rakes! The very best pruning shears, several kinds, and keep them sharp!*
>
> *So these years it's house and dinners and garden. If Maybeck had known I would live so long he would have built us a house without stairs and not on this steep lot. But he did and we had it and I love it.*[31]
>
> *We have never changed it—2751 [High House] is as tight and compact as a nut.*[32]

On the last page of her memoir, Jackie names all nine of her great-grandchildren, including "a crowning glory" of twins. "I've been down to see them, and I try to help. So much work. . . . Eat and sleep, cry a bit, be rocked. What a life!"[33]

In the autumn of 1995, Jackie added a chairlift to her stairs and hired an assistant, Joanna Volz. Joanna later told me:

> *Jackie had me build a fire every morning before she came upstairs riding her chair lift—she liked to hear and*

smell the fire first thing. She always looked like the sun coming up when she ascended in that chair, her white hair against the dark wood. She insisted on the fire no matter the weather, no matter if the wood was green. She had me burn any and everything: old brooms, yard-sticks, dried out ivy cuttings.

Jackie's mind was razor sharp and she seemingly remembered everything. She'd sit on an outdoor couch and orchestrate my weeding.[34]

In her final weeks, Jackie's bed was moved upstairs where she settled under the great northern window, close to her beloved fireplace. When I'd visit, she'd be drawing and writing in her journal, greeting visitors from her bed, offering a cup of tea. She died at home on August 17, 1996, at the age of ninety-five, surrounded by family. Robin Pennell, anticipating an end, came down the Drive from his home up the street, hurrying up the back pathway into the great room. "I just put my arms around Cherry. Jacomena had been such a part of this hill—that was an awful loss."[35]

We attended the memorial in Jackie's lower garden. The Maybeck Twin Drive Association planted a cherry tree in her honor on an island of the Drive, and we recently added a plaque with the inscription, "Jacomena van Huizen Maybeck 1901–1996. She loved cats, fine glazes, and especially her neighbors. Jackie, we'll never forget your grace, humor, and generosity."[36]

Jackie lived simply, marking the seasons, compromising with the Family and the deer, and inspiring so many of us who loved her. She was an immigrant who had longed for and finally created a home of her own.

I would miss chatting by phone or sharing tea with Jackie while discussing teenage behavior, college applications, and what makes a good photograph. She was perennially optimistic and supportive, encouraging me to go back to school at age fifty, as she had done. She loved being outdoors, noting the smallest early bud or change in the weather—reminding me now, as I write this, to notice these simple pleasures. The weather, she felt, really should be warmer, and it would be better if High House were on one level. In her late years, Jackie told me,

> *My desire has always been to be a well-rounded person, and that's not always easy. But you can still work at it. I had a wonderful background and upbringing. I'm still bouncing on the ranch with the sun and health I grew up with.*

"Sliding Home"

Photograph courtesy of Maybeck family.

Sifting through boxes of scrapbooks and photos, Jackie's granddaughter, Katherine, found a poem written in Jackie's hand in pencil on yellowed paper:

Youngness

What a lilting lovely thing is life
I'll drink to the very last drop.
Then hold the glass against the sky
It's empty I needs must stop.

I want to taste it truly and full
The part that is called my share
Age comes when appreciation has gone
And zest is no longer there.

I want to play while the playing is good
Drink deep of sun and air
Keep my heart light and my laughing free
And shoulder my burdens of care.

I want my place in the newness of things
In love and the songs that are sung
The sport and sweetness and circus to jest
That were since time was young.

And when death rings the curtain down
We've fulfilled and enjoyed our part—
We've gloried in things that were made for our joy
Unafraid; young in heart.[37]

Jacomena and Toby, 1980.

Photograph courtesy of Maybeck family.

EPILOGUE

Lloyd and I are hoping to live in High House until they carry us out. Sitting in my rocking chair, I gaze out windows that summon me outdoors to the trees, birds, and deer, just as Maybeck had intended. Being in the house comforts us. We live a simpler lifestyle style now, with fewer objects, longer walks, more time for friends and family . . . and we're finally using (and chipping) our celadon bowls signed by Jacomena. It's a life we savor.

Although High House will always be known as "Jackie's house," we've put our stamp on it too, recently adding curtains. The drafty porch is now a proper kitchen; and Jackie's studio has been rebuilt as Lloyd's office. It's warm and cozy and made of wood, not cinderblock. But it's still called the Pot Shop, and Lloyd says it's a fine place for being creative. The double railing on the stairway to the great room supports our old knees, and the vestiges of Jackie's garden greet us every morning at breakfast.

Pepe looks longingly across the road to the Cottage, perhaps remembering his youth.

In early 2019, Lloyd, my friend Susan, and I headed back to Pine Ridge Road, determined to finally find the old van Huizen ranch. It's now owned by Erich Pearson, an early proponent and lobbyist for medical marijuana, and managed by his brother, Alex. They kindly invited us to visit. Passing through padlocked gates and fording Robinson Creek, we found ourselves on Jackie's narrow and muddy "string bean road,"[1] climbing to a flat knoll. And there it was: the original house was still standing, dwarfed by a huge redwood, just as Noni and Jerry Chaney had promised. I was overwhelmed—I could barely speak. In all these years, I had never imagined that the old house would still be there. The original 1916 pine poles still hold up the roof, and Piet's cabin still has the best view of the countryside and the small (now legal) marijuana farm below. Wandering the warren of rustic rooms reminded me of those Maybeck homes where sheds and porches were added as needed. I stood by the small woodstove in the main room, imagining Jackie huddled there with her mother after dinner. Finding the ranch felt like an ending for me. Memories of Jackie will endure, like this old house.

Despite the beauty and peacefulness of the land where "dreams were dreamed and hearts grew warm to each other,"[2] I could understand why Jackie left it. Without a family or her first soul mate—her mother—the land would have felt too remote and isolated. And lonely. And it was a long way from Berkeley.

The van Huizen ranch house and Loki, 2019.

Photograph by Pam Valois.

Left to right: Susan Kanaan and Pam Valois at the van Huizen ranch house, 2019.

Photograph by Lloyd Linford.

NAMES AND ADDRESSES OF HOUSES DESCRIBED IN THIS STORY

The names and addresses of houses described in this story are in chronological order. All houses are located in Berkeley, California, except #2 and #8.

1. **2701 Buena Vista Way:** built in 1907 by Bernard Maybeck as his family home. It was destroyed in the 1923 Berkeley fire. (The address, 2701, is now that of the William and Kerna Maybeck Gannon House, built in 1959 by Reece Clark.)
2. **The van Huizen ranch,** acquired in 1913, is ten miles west of Ukiah, now at 5000 Knoxville Road, a small road off of Pine Ridge Road.
3. **2711 Buena Vista Way:** built in 1924 by Bernard Maybeck for his son, Wallen. It is called the Maybeck Studio or Sack House.
4. **1 Maybeck Twin Drive:** built in 1926 by Bernard Maybeck for himself and his wife, Annie, after the

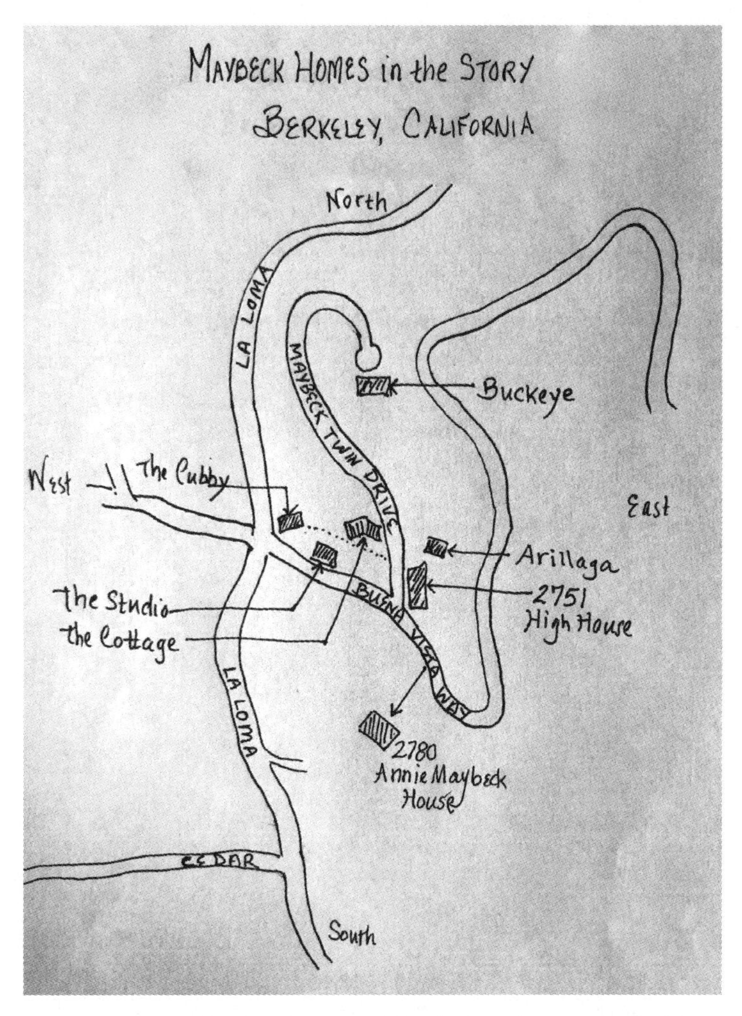

Houses described in this story, Berkeley, California, 2020.

Drawing by Pam Valois.

1923 fire destroyed his previous home at 2701 Buena Vista Way. It is called the Maybeck Cottage. Before Maybeck Twin Drive was created, the address of the Cottage was 2745 Buena Vista Way.

5. **1471 La Loma Avenue:** built in 1926 by Bernard Maybeck as a garage; an addition was added in 1930. It is called the Cubby House.
6. **2751 Buena Vista Way:** built in 1932 by Bernard Maybeck for his son, Wallen, and family. It is called High House, or the Wallen Maybeck House #1.
7. **2780 Buena Vista Way:** built in 1932 by Bernard Maybeck for himself and his wife, Annie, and for their daughter, Kerna, when she married. It is variously called the Annie Maybeck House, Kerna's House, or Annie's House.
8. **135 Purdue Avenue, Kensington, California:** built in 1937 by Bernard Maybeck for Wallen Maybeck and his family. It is called Hilltop or the Wallen Maybeck House #2.
9. **2 Maybeck Twin Drive:** built in 1950 by Bernard Maybeck with Wallen and Jacomena Maybeck. It is called Arillaga.
10. **2885 Buena Vista Way:** built in 1959 by Wallen and Jacomena Maybeck. It is called Buckeye House. The driveway is at the top of Maybeck Twin Drive.

NOTES

Prologue: pages xi–xxi

1. Several houses are mentioned in this story; see Names and Addresses of Houses Described in this story, 204.
2. Alan Temko, "Introduction," in *Maybeck: The Family View* (Berkeley, CA: Berkeley Architectural Heritage Association, 1979).
3. Jacomena Maybeck, interview by Pamela Valois and Charlotte Painter, October 1980, 2751 Buena Vista Way, Berkeley, CA. Unpublished.
4. Jacomena Maybeck, "A Season-by-Season Recounting of the City of Trees," *Independent and Gazette* (Berkeley, CA), June 3, 1981.
5. Jacqueline Schmeal, "The House Maybeck Built," *Christian Science Monitor*, July 29, 1970.
6. Charlotte Painter and Pamela Valois, *Gifts of Age: Portraits and Essays of 32 Remarkable Women* (San Francisco, CA: Chronicle Books, 1985).
7. Jacomena Maybeck, *People & Places: A Memoir* (Berkeley, CA: Stonegarden Press, 1992), 145.
8. Jacomena Maybeck, *Maybeck: The Family View* (Berkeley, CA: Berkeley Architectural Heritage Association, 1980).

9. Florence Jury and Jacomena Maybeck, *The 4-Year Stretch* (Berkeley, CA: self-published, 1979), Pamela Valois's Papers, Berkeley, CA. (The original title is: *The 4-YEAR STRETCH.*)
10. Mary Jane Moffat and Charlotte Painter, *Revelations: Diaries of Women* (New York: Random House, Inc., 1974).

Chapter One: A Magic Place, pages 3–20.

1. Maybeck, *People & Places*, 1. (Here Jackie spells it Rensius; it is written as Renzius in his obituary.)
2. Jacomena Maybeck, "The Dutch Family History" (unpublished manuscript, 1986), Family Papers, Adriana Nittler, Santa Cruz, CA.
3. Maybeck, *People & Places*, 9.
4. Ibid., 11.
5. Ibid., 10.
6. Anthony Bruce, "Maybeck Country: Hillside Houses of the Early- and Mid-20th Century," Berkeley Architectural Heritage Association Newsletter (Berkeley, CA, 2009): 1. For more information on Bernard Maybeck, see Bibliography.
7. Maybeck, *Family View*, 11. In this quotation, Kleyn-Schoorel is misspelled ("Klein"), and "van Huizen" is written Van Huizen.
8. Maybeck, *People & Places*, 16.
9. Ibid., 18.
10. Jury and Maybeck, *4-Year Stretch*, 10.
11. Maybeck, *People & Places*, 11.
12. Ibid., 20.
13. Anabel Cole, interview by Pamela Valois, 2016, Berkeley, CA.
14. Jury and Maybeck, *4-Year Stretch*, 10.

15. *Ukiah Republican Press* (Ukiah, CA), December 26, 1913.
16. Jury and Maybeck, *4-Year Stretch*, 10.
17. Ibid., 10–11.
18. Jacomena Maybeck, personal diary, August 1930, Family Papers, Nittler.
19. Ibid.
20. Ibid.
21. Jury and Maybeck, *4-Year Stretch*, 36.
22. Maybeck, *People & Places, 26.*
23. *Ukiah Dispatch Democrat* (Ukiah, CA), June 24, 1921.
24. Maybeck, *People & Places*, 27.
25. Jury and Maybeck, *4-Year Stretch*, 3.
26. Maybeck, *People & Places*, 29.
27. Maybeck, *Family View*, 17.
28. Robin Pennell, interview by Lloyd Linford, 2017, Berkeley, CA. Sadly, Robin died December 21, 2020.

Chapter Two: Learning a Way of Life, pages 21–34.

1. Jury and Maybeck, *4-Year Stretch*, 3.
2. Ibid., 2.
3. Maybeck, *People & Places*, 31.
4. Jury and Maybeck, *4-Year Stretch*, 16.
5. Ibid., 9.
6. Ibid., 6.
7. Maybeck, *People & Places*, 40.
8. Kerna Maybeck to Annie Maybeck, September 1923, Bancroft Library, UC Berkeley, CA. BANC MSS 88/21 C Box 1, CB782.
9. Mira A. Maclay, "The Maybeck One-Room House," in *The Early Sunset Magazine 1898–1928*, ed. Paul C. Johnson (San Francisco, CA: California Historical Society, 1973), 199–201.

10. Jury and Maybeck, *4-Year Stretch*, 14.
11. Maybeck, *People & Places*, 36.
12. Jury and Maybeck, *4-Year Stretch*, 10.
13. Maybeck, *People & Places*, 45.
14. Jury and Maybeck, *4-Year Stretch*, 7.
15. Ibid., 15.
16. Ibid., 34.
17. Ibid., 36.
18. Ibid., 36.
19. Ibid., 45.
20. Sheila Bathurst, interview by Pamela Valois, March 2017, Issaquah, WA, with daughters Katherine Sorensen and Adrienne McGuire. Sadly, Sheila died in February 2019 in Seattle just before her ninetieth birthday.
21. Jury and Maybeck, *4-Year Stretch*, 11.
22. Ibid., 21.
23. Ibid., 43.
24. Ibid., 43.
25. Florence Jury, "The Lighter Side of the Depression," in *Exactly Opposite the Golden Gate: Essays on Berkeley's History 1845–1945*, ed. Phil McArdle (Berkeley, CA: The Berkeley Historical Society, 1983), 350–351.
26. Maybeck, *Family View*, 18–20.
27. Jury and Maybeck, *4-Year Stretch*, 51.

Chapter Three: Full Tilt into Life, pages 37–68.

1. Family Papers, Katherine Sorensen, Issaquah, WA.
2. J. Maybeck, personal diary, June 1927.
3. Ibid.
4. Ibid.
5. Jacomena van Huizen to Wallen Maybeck, August 13, 1927, Family Papers, Sorensen. Letter sent from

Portland, Oregon, to Wallen Maybeck's office in San Francisco, CA; six handwritten pages, excerpted here.

6. Maybeck, *People & Places*, 45–46.
7. Maybeck, *Family View*, 1. Jacomena and Wallen were married September 6, 1927.
8. Maybeck, *People & Places*, 39.
9. Jury and Maybeck, *4-Year Stretch*, 51.
10. The Ranch Log: a record of the comings and goings of visitors to the van Huizen ranch from December 1927 to September 1936. It includes sketches and notes by Jacomena and Wallen Maybeck, Helene van Huizen, and visitors, with a summary of events from 1936 to 1950. The Log, "a register for those who shall taste of the simple life on Pine Ridge," was given to Pieter and Helene van Huizen by Fran Uridge. Family Papers, Nittler.
11. Ranch Log, September 1934.
12. Wallen Maybeck, "A Hunting Season Honeymoon," Family Papers, Sorensen.
13. Maybeck, *People & Places*, 52.
14. Annie Maybeck to Jacomena Maybeck, n.d., Family Papers, Sorensen. The letter was sent from Los Angeles where Ben Maybeck was hospitalized in the winter of 1928.
15. Maybeck, *People & Places*, 52.
16. Maybeck, *Family View*, 21. Ben was working on a house for Earl. C. Anthony; he later recovered from an infection following prostate surgery, staying in a sanitarium in Los Angeles with Annie nearby.
17. Kerna Maybeck to Jacomena Maybeck, 1929, Family Papers, Sorensen.
18. Adriana (Cherry) Nittler, interview by Pamela Valois, October 2016, Santa Cruz, CA, with son, Scott Nittler,

and daughter, Sheila K. Connelly. Cherry celebrated her ninetieth birthday in March 2019.

19. Jacomena van Huizen to Wallen Maybeck, August 13, 1927 (see chap. 3, n. 5).
20. Ranch Log, September 1929.
21. Maybeck, *People & Places*, 45.
22. Katherine Sorensen, interview by Pamela Valois, October 2017, Issaquah, WA.
23. Adriana Nittler, interview by Pamela Valois.
24. Maybeck, *People & Places*, 58.
25. Maybeck, *Family View*, 21.
26. Kerna Gannon to Jacomena Maybeck, January 1975, Family Papers, Sorensen.
27. Ranch Log, April 1930.
28. Ibid., August 1930.
29. Jacomena Maybeck, "The JacandWallen House" (unpublished manuscript, 1995), Family Papers, Adriana Nittler, Santa Cruz, CA.
30. Maybeck, *People & Places*, 51.
31. Jury and Maybeck, *4-Year Stretch*, 50.
32. Ranch Log, December 1930.
33. Wallen Maybeck to Annie Maybeck, October 16, 1930, Bernard Maybeck Collection, Environmental Design Archives, UC Berkeley, Maybeck, B. file 1956-1. Correspondence—Family, 1925–1930 N.D., Box CB782, folder 1.
34. Jacomena Maybeck to Helene van Huizen, January 6, 1931, Family Papers, Sorensen.
35. Jacomena Maybeck to the Family [Ben and Annie Maybeck], August 30, 1931, Family Papers, Sorensen.
36. Adriana Nittler's talk at the Berkeley City Club, n.d., Family Papers, Nittler. The talk may have been in 1957

when the club was still called the Berkeley Women's City Club.

37. Adriana Nittler, interview by Pamela Valois.
38. Sheila Bathurst, interview by Pamela Valois.
39. Bernard Maybeck to Adriana and Sheila Maybeck, 1933, Family Papers, Sorensen.
40. Robin Pennell, interview by Pamela Valois, January 2017, Berkeley, CA.
41. Maybeck, *Family View*, 20.
42. J. Maybeck, personal diary, August 20, 1932.
43. Sheila Bathurst, interview by Pamela Valois.
44. Adriana Nittler, interview by Pamela Valois.
45. Ranch Log, September 1931.
46. Ibid., October 1931.
47. J. Maybeck to Kerna Maybeck, August 1931, Family Papers, Sorensen.

Chapter Four: A Home of Their Own, pages 69–91.

1. Robert M. Craig, *Bernard Maybeck at the Principia College: The Art and Craft of Building* (Layton, Utah: Gibbs Smith, 2004), xxii (Annie Maybeck's letter to Frederic E. Morgan, February 27, 1944).
2. Ibid., 57. Frederic E. Morgan, "Report of Progress on College Plans," April 25, 1930, and Helena C. Gunnison, "Report to the Trustees of The Principia," late March 1932.
3. Bruce, "Maybeck Country," Berkeley Architectural Heritage Association Newsletter (2009).
4. Sheila Bathurst, interview by Pamela Valois.
5. Maybeck, *Family View*, 29.
6. Blake Edgar, "The Gospel According to Maybeck," *Express, The East Bay's Free Weekly* (Berkeley, CA), Volume 13, No. 8: 39, November 1990.

7. Jacomena Maybeck, "Cat's-eye View of Life at the Cottage," *Independent and Gazette* (Berkeley, CA), April 9, 1981. Commentary by "Snoops" and "Sam" as told to Jacomena Maybeck for the Berkeley Architectural Heritage Association.
8. Craig, *Bernard Maybeck at the Principia College*, 79. (Frederic E. Morgan interview conducted by Charles B. Hosmer Jr., Elsah, IL, September 4, 1970.)
9. The Hillside Club was founded in 1898. Its mission was "to protect the hills of Berkeley from unsightly grading and the building of unsuitable and disfiguring houses." Among the legacies of the club are North Berkeley's curved streets with old trees, walking paths, and numerous small parks. As time passed, the club changed its emphasis to include dramatic presentations and a broader range of cultural events. Today, the Hillside Club provides historical perspective and a sense of community through its social and cultural events.
10. Untitled booklet, Hillside Club (Berkeley, CA), 1906.
11. Charles Keeler, *The Simple Home* (San Francisco, CA: Smith Elder and Co., 1904).
12. Ranch Log, September 1932.
13. In the spring of 1932, Bernard Maybeck was juggling plans for the two Berkeley hillside houses with the momentous task of supervising construction on the college campus of Principia. But by October 1932, Principia construction was halted for a year by the Principia Board of Trustees due to labor strikes and controversy over architectural expenses and inadequate funds. Ben and Annie spent two weeks in October 1932 touring Principia's deserted site, and did not return to Illinois until October 1933. We can therefore guess that Ben was back on-site in

Berkeley, either that fall of 1932, or in early 1933, supervising construction of 2751 and 2780, working around the rainy months.

14. Jacomena Maybeck, "A Stroll through the Gateways of the City," *Independent and Gazette* (Berkeley, CA), November 12, 1980.
15. J. Maybeck to Mr. Limerick, January 28, 1977, Family Papers, Sorensen.
16. John Ribovich, "In the Heart of Maybeck Country: Berkeley's Wallen Maybeck House," *American Bungalow* 64, (2009): 41. "Here, Maybeck used a device also favored by Wright: making a grand space seem even grander by causing one to enter it from a smaller, humbler one."
17. Charles Duncan, "A Vision for the Ages, Part I," Scholars' Essays, The Maybeck Foundation, accessed June 18, 2019, www.maybeck.org.
18. Adriana Nittler, interview by Pamela Valois.
19. Gerald Adams, "The Maybeck Environment," *San Francisco Sunday Examiner and Chronicle*, (San Francisco, CA), December 5, 1976.
20. Jury, "The Lighter Side of the Depression," 351.
21. J. Maybeck to Siegfried Brockmann, June 20, 1994, A. Bruce Papers, Berkeley, CA.
22. Maybeck, *People & Places*, 62.
23. Maybeck, "JacandWallen House."
24. Jury, "The Lighter Side of the Depression," 351–352.
25. Ibid., 352–353.
26. Ranch Log, December 1934.
27. J. Maybeck, personal diary, August 1931.
28. Maybeck, *People & Places*, 62.
29. Annie Maybeck to Wallen Maybeck, December 1, 1933, Family Papers, Sorensen. Excerpted from a 24-page letter

from "Little Grannie" (Annie Maybeck) to "Darling Wallen," written from Principia College in Illinois.

30. J. Maybeck, personal diary, October 1937.
31. Maybeck, *Family View*, 23–24.
32. Sheila Bathurst, interview by Pamela Valois.
33. Robin Pennell, interview by Pamela Valois, 2017. Robin turned ninety in 2018, celebrating at a happy neighborhood party at the Cottage, graced by his childhood friend, Cherry Maybeck Nittler, and her family.
34. Ibid.
35. Sheila Bathurst, interview by Pamela Valois.
36. Ranch Log, November 1935.
37. J. Maybeck, personal diary, August 24, 1932.
38. Maybeck, *People & Places*, 65.
39. Sheila Bathurst, interview by Pamela Valois.
40. Jacomena Maybeck, "Elegant House Essay" (unpublished manuscript, 1936), Family Papers, Nittler.
41. Maybeck, *People & Places*, 67.
42. Ibid., 67.
43. Tillie Olsen, *Silences* (New York: Delacorte Press/Seymour Lawrence, 1978), 33.

Chapter Five: Another House, Another Fire, pages 92–101.

1. Maybeck, *Family View*, 31.
2. Maybeck, *People & Places*, 68.
3. Adriana Nittler, interview by Pamela Valois.
4. Ibid.
5. J. Maybeck, personal diary, November 1937.
6. Ibid., November 1937.
7. J. Maybeck to Mr. Limerick, January 28, 1977.
8. Bernard Maybeck was awarded the Gold Medal of Honor by the American Institute of Architects in 1951.

His son, Wallen Maybeck, attended in his place and gave the acceptance speech. Family Papers, Nittler.

9. Adriana Nittler, interview by Pamela Valois.
10. J. Maybeck, personal diary, January 1948.
11. Ibid.
12. Ibid., January 1938.
13. Ibid., October 1938.
14. Richard Ward, interview by Pamela Valois, 2018, Walnut Creek, CA.
15. *Berkeley Daily Gazette*, Saturday Evening Edition, October 15, 1938. Archives are currently housed in the Berkeley Architectural Heritage Association office, Berkeley, CA.
16. Ibid.
17. Sheila Bathurst, interview by Pamela Valois.
18. Richard Ward, interview by Pamela Valois.
19. Richard Ward to George Schuetz, February 1, 2012, Pamela Valois's Papers.
20. Even now, at 2751 Buena Vista Way, sand occasionally trickles down from the rafters.

Chapter Six: Following Daddy, pages 102–108.

1. Sheila Bathurst, interview by Pamela Valois.
2. Adriana Nittler, interview by Pamela Valois.
3. Maybeck, *People & Places*, 79–80.
4. Ibid., 84.
5. Maybeck, *People & Places*, 87.
6. Katherine Sorensen, interview by Pamela Valois.
7. Adriana Nittler, interview by Pamela Valois.
8. Ibid.
9. Sheila Bathurst, interview by Pamela Valois.
10. Maybeck, *People & Places*, 91.
11. J. Maybeck to Mr. Limerick, January 28, 1977.

12. Maybeck, *Family View*, 34.
13. Sheila Bathurst, interview by Pamela Valois.
14. Robert Kehlmann, "Jaime de Angulo, Anthropologist, 'Erratic Genius,'" (2015): www.berkeleyplaques.org.
15. Charles Wollenburg, *Berkeley: A City in History* (Berkeley, CA: University of California Press, 2007), 76.
16. Ed Herny, Shelley Rideout, and Katie Wadell, *Berkeley Bohemia: Artists and Visionaries of the Early 20th Century* (Layton, Utah: Gibbs Smith, 2008), Dust Jacket.
17. Katherine Sorensen, interview by Pamela Valois.

Chapter Seven: Jackie as Em, pages 111–129.

1. Jacomena Maybeck, "Journey: Small Adventure" (unpublished manuscript, 1952), Family Papers, Sorensen. The front flap reads "Title: Journey, JM. 1946. To Sheila and John, in memory of 1947. Jacomena, Berkeley." A letter dated February 20, 1976, found inside Sheila Bathurst's copy reads:

   Dear Charles,
   This diary has been lying in my cedar chest since—maybe 1948. We went to Germany in Sept. 1946 and home 1947 to CCAC 1948—I think! As I re-read I find many mistakes in the typing. I had it done. But here is our war story and my re-actions to Paris and Germany. I've never shown it to anyone—it's saved for the twins—I've only 2 copies. Jackie.

2. J. Maybeck, personal diary, January 10, 1938.
3. Ibid., July 18, 1946.
4. Maybeck, *People & Places*, 99.
5. Maybeck, "The JacandWallen House."

Chapter Eight: Freedom and Loss, pages 130–146.

1. Ranch Log, postscript by Jacomena Maybeck, 1953.
2. Sheila Bathurst, interview by Pamela Valois.
3. Maybeck, "Dutch Family History."
4. *Ukiah News* (Ukiah, CA), October 22, 1953. Pieter van Huizen was born February 11, 1869, in Holland; died October 12, 1953, at his ranch near Ukiah.
5. Adriana Nittler, "The Pine Ridge Road" (unpublished manuscript, n.d.), Family Papers, Sorensen.
6. "Mory" was Morfydd Cardell who was married to Knox Cardell. Noni Chaney believes they owned the van Huizen ranch at some point.
7. Ranch Log, postscript by Jacomena Maybeck, 1953.
8. Maybeck, *People & Places*, 112–113.
9. Maybeck, *Family View*, 36.
10. Maybeck, *People & Places*, 118–120.
11. Robin Pennell, interview by Pamela Valois.
12. Maybeck, *People & Places*, 121.
13. Ibid., 116.
14. Ibid., 116.
15. Maybeck, *People & Places*, 122–123.
16. Maybeck, *Family View*, 38.
17. J. Maybeck to Mr. Limerick, January 28, 1977.
18. Sheila Bathurst, interview by Pamela Valois.
19. Maybeck, *People & Places*, 125.
20. Ibid., 65.
21. Ibid., 127.
22. Ibid., 128–129.

Chapter Nine: Just Jackie, pages 149–165.

1. Adriana Nittler, interview by Pamela Valois.
2. Yukako Okudaira, email message to Pamela Valois, 2016.

3. J. Maybeck to Sheila & John Bathhurst, April 1963, Family Papers, Sorensen.
4. Yukako Okudaira, telephone interview by Pamela Valois, July 11, 2016.
5. J. Maybeck to S. & J. Bathurst, April 1963.
6. Ibid., January 18, 1962.
7. Ibid., April 15, 1963. Sent from Hawaii, en route from Japan.
8. Maybeck, *People & Places*, 131–133.
9. J. Maybeck to S. Bathurst, September 1963, Family Papers, Sorensen.
10. Ibid., September 4, 1963.
11. Ibid., June 9, 1964.
12. Ibid., 1963.
13. J. Maybeck to S. & J. Bathurst, January 16, 1963.
14. Ibid., December 30, 1962.
15. Victor Seeger, interview by Pamela Valois, 2017, Berkeley, CA.
16. J. Maybeck to S. & J. Bathurst, October 28, 1963.
17. Ibid., June 5, 1964.
18. J. Maybeck to J. Bathurst, October 23, 1963.
19. J. Maybeck to Siegfried Brockmann, June 20, 1994.
20. Sheila Bathurst, interview by Pamela Valois.
21. Ibid.
22. Katherine Sorensen, "Images of a Woman" (unpublished manuscript, 1975), written in English 271, Washington State University, Family Papers, Katherine Sorensen.
23. J. Maybeck, "The patchwork cottage as seen through a cat's eye," *Independent and Gazette* (Berkeley, CA), April 21, 1981. Commentary by Albert and Alvin as told to Jacomena Maybeck for the Berkeley Architectural Heritage Association.

24. J. Maybeck to Kerna Maybeck, n.d., Family Papers, Sorensen.
25. Annie Cole, interview by Pamela Valois, 2017, Berkeley, CA.
26. J. Maybeck, "The patchwork cottage."
27. Ibid.

Chapter Ten: Savoring the Gifts of Age, pages 166–199.

1. Jury and Maybeck, *4-Year Stretch*, 36.
2. Maybeck, *People & Places*, 145–6.
3. J. Maybeck to Adriana Nittler, April 1980, Family Papers, Sorensen.
4. J. Maybeck, "A Season-by-Season Recounting of the City of Trees," *Independent and Gazette* (Berkeley, CA), June 3, 1981.
5. Susan Sontag, essay in the *New York Review of Books*, 1973.
6. M. F. K. Fisher (Mary Frances Kennedy Fisher, 1908–1992) interview by Pamela Valois, 1981, Valley of the Moon, Glen Ellen, CA.
7. Maybeck, *People & Places*, 147.
8. Adriana Nittler, "Jacomena, A Mother Who Leads the Way," *Santa Cruz Sentinel* (Santa Cruz, CA), May 11, 1980.
9. J. Maybeck, "The Small House," (unpublished manuscript, 1979), Pamela Valois's Papers, Berkeley, CA.
10. J. Maybeck, "The patchwork cottage."
11. Ibid.
12. Scott Nittler, interview by Pamela Valois, 2017, Berkeley, CA.
13. Maybeck, *People & Places*, 144.
14. Dan McGuire, interview by Pamela Valois, 2017, Berkeley, CA.

15. Adrienne McGuire, interview by Pamela Valois, 2017, Berkeley, CA.
16. Ibid.
17. Alan Temko, "Introduction," in *Maybeck: The Family View*, 1979.
18. Bernard Maybeck was born in 1862 in New York, the son of German immigrants.
19. Julia Child, interview by Pamela Valois, 1980, Santa Barbara, CA.
20. Jon Rantzman, interview by Pamela Valois, June 2017, Walnut Creek, CA.
21. Ibid.
22. Siegfried Brockmann, interview by Pamela Valois, 2017, Berkeley, CA.
23. Roger Raiche, email message to Pamela Valois, 2017. Roger was the horticulturist in charge of the California collection at the University of California Botanical Gardens (Berkeley, CA) and rented the Maybeck Cottage in 1988; he bought it in 1999.
24. J. Maybeck to S. Bathurst, April 30, 1980. Numbers 7 and 8 were not listed!
25. Ibid., May 31, 1981.
26. Ibid., October 12, 1981.
27. Ibid., December 7, 1981.
28. Ibid., January 9, 1982.
29. J. Maybeck to Yukako Okudaira, December 31, 1990, Y. Okudaira's Papers, New York, NY.
30. Anthony Bruce, interview by Pamela Valois, 2017, Berkeley, CA.
31. Maybeck, *People & Places*, 146–147.
32. J. Maybeck to Mr. Limerick, January 28, 1977.
33. Maybeck, *People & Places*, 148.

34. Joanna Volz, email message to Pamela Valois, 2016.
35. Robin Pennell, interview by Pamela Valois.
36. The Maybeck Twin Drive Association voted in April 2015 to install a memorial plaque to Jacomena Maybeck beneath the cherry tree planted many years ago in her honor on the lower island of Maybeck Twin Drive. It was designed and installed by Lloyd Linford and Jana Olson for the association in 2017. Lucy, the current cat living at #1 Maybeck Twin Drive, stopped by for the ceremony.
37. *Youngness*, n.d., Family Papers, Sorensen. It is not known whether Jackie composed this poem or copied it.

Epilogue: pages 201–203.

1. Jury and Maybeck, *4-Year Stretch*, 11.
2. The Ranch Log, postscript by Jacomena Maybeck, 1953.

SELECTED BIBLIOGRAPHY: BOOKS, MAGAZINES, NEWSLETTERS, AND WEBSITES

Berkeley Architectural Heritage Association. *Maybeck Country: Hillside Houses of the Early and Mid-20th Century*. Berkeley, CA: Berkeley Architectural Heritage Association, 2009.

Berkeley Architectural Heritage Association. *The 1923 Fire*. Berkeley, CA: Berkeley Architectural Heritage Association, 1992.

Cardwell, Kenneth H. *Bernard Maybeck: Artisan, Architect, Artist*. Salt Lake City: Peregrine Smith, Inc., 1977, reprinted by Hennessey + Ingalls, 1996.

Craig, Robert. *Bernard Maybeck at Principia College: The Art & Craft of Building*. Layton, Utah: Gibbs Smith, 2004.

Freudenheim, Leslie. *Building with Nature: Inspiration for the Arts and Crafts Home*. Layton, Utah: Gibbs Smith, 2005.

Harris, Dianne. *Maybeck's Landscapes: Drawing in Nature*. San Francisco, CA: William Stout, 2004.

Herny, Ed, Shelley Rideout, and Katie Wadell. *Berkeley Bohemia: Artists and Visionaries of the Early 20th Century*. Layton, Utah: Gibbs Smith, 2008.

Hosmer, Charles B. Jr. *Guidebook: Bernard Maybeck and Principia College, The Historic District*. Illinois: Principia College, 1998.

Johnson, Paul. C., ed., *The Early Sunset Magazine 1898–1928*. San Francisco & San Marino, CA: California Historical Society, 1973.

Jury, Florence, and Jacomena Maybeck. *The 4-YEAR STRETCH*. Berkeley, CA: Self-published, 1979.

Keeler, Charles A. *The Simple Home*. San Francisco, CA: Paul Elder and Co., 1904.

Maybeck, Jacomena. *Maybeck: The Family View*. Berkeley, CA: Berkeley Architectural Heritage Association, 1980.

Maybeck, Jacomena. *People & Places: A Memoir*. Berkeley, CA: Stonegarden Press, 1992.

McArdle, Phil, ed., *Exactly Opposite the Golden Gate: Essays on Berkeley's History 1845–1945*. Berkeley, CA: The Berkeley Historical Society, 1983.

McCoy, Esther. *Five California Architects*. New York: Reinholt Book Corp., 1960, reprinted by Praeger, 1970, and Hennessey & Ingalls, 1987.

Moffat, Mary Jane, and Charlotte Painter. *Revelations: Diaries of Women*. New York: Random House Inc., 1974.

Olsen, Tillie. *Silences*. New York: Delacorte Press, 1965, 1972, 1978.

Painter, Charlotte, and Pamela Valois. *Gifts of Age: Portraits and Essays of 32 Remarkable Women*. San Francisco, CA: Chronicle Books, 1985.

Ribovich, John. "In the Heart of Maybeck Country: Berkeley's Wallen Maybeck House." *American Bungalow*, no. 64 (Winter 2009): 34–47.

Wilson, Mark A. *Bernard Maybeck: Architect of Elegance*. Layton, Utah: Gibbs Smith, 2011.

Wollenberg, Charles. *Berkeley: A City in History*, Berkeley & Los Angeles, CA: University of California Press, 2008.
Woodbridge, Sally B. *Bernard Maybeck: Visionary Architect*. New York and London: Abbeville Press, 1992.

Berkeley Architectural Heritage Association:
http://www.berkeleyheritage.com

Berkeley Historical Society:
http.//www.berkeleyhistoricalsociety.org

California Historical Society:
https://californiahistoricalsociety.org

The Environmental Design Archives—University of California, Berkeley:
https://archives.ced.berkeley.edu.

Maybeck Foundation:
http://www.maybeck.org

Mendocino County Historical Society:
http://mendohistoricalsociety.com/index.html

ACKNOWLEDGMENTS

I am grateful to a community of friends and family who supported this project.

The story of Jacomena Maybeck unfolded on a lovely weekend in Seattle with Jackie's family. Her granddaughter, Katherine Sorensen, encouraged me to ransack her attic, unearthing unpublished photos and stories Jackie had written. A second granddaughter, Adrienne McGuire, and one of Jackie's twin daughters, Sheila Bathurst, joined us to share memories of Jackie over her favorite drink, Manhattans. In Santa Cruz, Cherry Nittler, Sheila's twin, lent me the ranch log detailing Jackie's sojourns to the ranch in her twenties and thirties, while Jackie's grandchildren, Scott Nittler and Sheila Connelly, searched drawers and closets, finding diaries and more photos. Thank you all for your generosity in helping me get this story into the world.

Chris Marino, curator of the UC Berkeley Environmental Design Archives, assisted me in sorting through many boxes of Maybeck family letters and gorgeous, huge drawings by Bernard Maybeck. Anthony Bruce, director of the Berkeley Architectural Heritage Association, tirelessly answered my questions about the history of Nut Hill and its houses. Thank you both.

As the story became a book, my husband, Lloyd Linford, was the first editor, helping me shape the material, offering encouragement and expertise. He could transform a convoluted sentence into a lovely one. Without him, there would be no book. Thank you from the bottom of my heart.

Susan Kanaan and I were college roommates and still savor get-togethers. Her second editing of the manuscript was invaluable at a time when I felt stuck. She sent me John McPhee's essay, "Draft No. 4," which immediately stopped my whining. Thank you so much, Susan.

A huge thank-you to friends who've politely asked, over the last four years, "How's the book going?" The answer was always the same—"I'm on my last draft!" Your interest and support has kept this project alive. Thank you, Connie Milligan, Sandi Blair, Marybeth Whittemore, Carol Cohen, Tim and Marian Nelson, Tal Harari, Tom Cohen, Julie and Neil Guiney, Maxine Berzok, Marj Wolf, Alta Tingle, John and Tina Gillis, Kathy Brown, Jim Bonde, Shorey and Lois Myers, Tom Turner, Andrea Paulos, Mara Salomon, and Annie Cole.

Neighbors had wonderful stories about Jackie and were eager to share them. Thank you, Robin Pennell, Victor Seeger, Roger Raiche, Siegfried Brockmann, Jon and Evelyn Rantzman, Brigitte McKenzie, and Joanna Volz.

A year ago, Tina Gillis read the story and wrote four pages of notes and considerations. After reading them, I thought I'd just quit while I was ahead, but she encouraged me to bring more of myself into the story, and eventually, I did. More importantly, she introduced me to She Writes Press. Thank you, Tina.

She Writes Press—it is hard to imagine a more collegial and educational sisterhood. Upon acceptance, I was invited to gatherings of SWP authors and to webinars about publishing and marketing a book. Not only is the publisher, Brooke Warner, available and supportive, but her dream of a "hybrid press" leads the industry with indie book awards. Thank you too, Samantha Strom, my responsive Editorial Project Manager.

More thank-yous to those who helped me along the way: Martha Casselman, my agent for *Gifts of Age*; Yukako Okudaira, Jackie's first boarder; Gina Campbell for the Pine Ridge Road adventures; Kristine of Spirit Chicken Farm for introductions to Erich and Alex; Noni and Jerry Chaney for the history of Pine Ridge Road; Marianna Ackerman for design advice; and Dan and Ade McGuire for stories about remodeling a house with Jackie. A special thanks to Richard and Jewell Ward who visited and told us things about our house we'd not known. Richard lived with the Maybecks in 1938, and helped fight the house fire. He emailed me last month reminding me to get this book out before he turns one hundred years old!

And finally, thank you to my family. If only Mom and Pop could be here now to celebrate.

My sons, Zack and Scott, and their partners, Rachel and Megan, dutifully appreciate the quirks of our wooden house; Abby and Joe find unusual hideouts for their games, and love curling up on the sofa with Lloyd to hear a story; Resa and David visit from Seattle; and Renee flies from Phoenix to make Thanksgiving gravy. We hope the house feels as welcoming to them as it always will be to us.

ABOUT THE AUTHOR

photo © Abby R. Linford

Growing up in Sierra Madre, California, Pamela Valois moved north to attend UC Berkeley during the Free Speech Movement. After almost flunking out due to political rallies and other interests—birth control pills had just been offered—she returned to Los Angeles to become a dental hygienist. Then, with a solid part-time job, she could enjoy being a quasi-hippie, selling macramé and her photos at weekend craft fairs. Pamela married psychologist Lloyd Linford on the lawn of Jacomena Maybeck's Berkeley cottage and studied photography with Ruth Bernhard in San Francisco. *Gifts of Age: Portraits and Essays of 32 Remarkable Women*, a best seller inspired by Jacomena, was published in 1985. After immensely enjoying mothering two sons, Pamela earned a master's degree and started a new career in health care. Now at age seventy-five, she's been retired for ten years. She enjoys walking in the woods, reading, and hanging out with friends and family. Pamela's grandchildren, Abby and Joe, are a great joy and require exploring things not done in years. Her daily pleasure is now living in Jacomena's High House with Lloyd—it's like a tree house, with redwoods, deer, and skunks as neighbors. Lloyd and Pamela meet after breakfast to discuss plans for the day, then retreat to their rooms to write until lunch. It's a life she savors.

Visit Pamela online at
https://pamvaloisbloominginwinter.com

SELECTED TITLES FROM SHE WRITES PRESS

She Writes Press is an independent publishing company founded to serve women writers everywhere. Visit us at www.shewritespress.com.

Love, Life, and Lucille: Lessons Learned from a Centenarian by Judy Gaman. $16.95, 978-1-63152-882-8. Judy, a feisty, forty-something professional trapped in the unrelenting world of workaholism, forges an incredible bond with a centenarian—and life takes on a whole new meaning for both of them.

Never Sit If You Can Dance: Lessons from My Mother by Jo Giese. $16.95, 978-1-63152-533-9. Babe was no goodie two-shoes: she drank, danced, and stayed up very late. She favored colorful clothes, liked giving parties, adored her husband, and always told her daughter, "Never sit if you can dance." Told with lighthearted good humor, this a charming tale of the way things used to be—and probably still should be.

Motherlines: Letters of Love, Longing, and Liberation by Patricia Reis. $16.95, 978-1-63152-121-8. In her midlife search for meaning, and longing for maternal connection, Patricia Reis encounters uncommon women who inspire her journey and discovers an unlikely confidante in her aunt, a free-spirited Franciscan nun.

Our Grand Finale: A Daughter's Memoir by Laraine Denny Burrell. $16.95, 978-1-63152-238-3. When Laraine Burrell's father dies unexpectedly, she is left bereft and guilt ridden, and questioning whether she made the right decision in leaving their home in England so many years before.

Naked Mountain: A Memoir by Marcia Mabee. $16.95, 978-1-63152-097-6. A compelling memoir of one woman's journey of natural world discovery, tragedy, and the enduring bonds of marriage, set against the backdrop of a stunning mountaintop in rural Virginia.

Implosion: Memoir of an Architect's Daughter by Elizabeth W. Garber. $16.95, 978-1-63152-351-9. When Elizabeth Garber, her architect father, and the rest of their family move into Woodie's modern masterpiece, a glass house, in 1966, they have no idea that over the next few years their family's life will be shattered—both by Woodie's madness and the turbulent 1970s.